Individualizing Learning through Modular-Flexible Programming

Individualizing Learning through Modular-Flexible Programming

Gaynor Petrequin
Principal, John Marshall High School
Portland, Oregon

McGraw-Hill Book Company
New York St. Louis San Francisco Toronto London Sydney

INDIVIDUALIZING LEARNING THROUGH
MODULAR-FLEXIBLE PROGRAMMING

Library of Congress Catalog Card Number 68–26567

1 2 3 4 5 6 7 8 9 0 V B V B 7 5 4 3 2 1 0 6 9 8

Foreword

Within broad state and local requirements and laws, a school faculty in Portland has the freedom to decide what to teach and how to teach. Instructional decisions thus can be made close to the students they will affect, and each school can become a laboratory for the testing of educational ideas and designs.

Marshall High School, under the direction of Principal Gaynor Petrequin, has become such a laboratory. Marshall is exercising its freedom in a creative search for better ways to organize space and time for students. The techniques in use at Marshall, and some tentative conclusions regarding them, are explained in this book.

The basis for all phases of the Marshall Program is found in the recognition that each student does, and must do, his own learning. No one can learn for him. The whole of the program at Marshall is an attempt to individualize instruction—to organize the instructional program so that each of Marshall's 2,200 students is able to adjust the program to fit his individual needs. It is the curriculum that is adapted to the student, rather than the student who is made to fit the curriculum.

Of course, implementation of the program at Marshall—with its diversity of class periods, student schedules, and teacher assignments—would be impracticable, if not impossible, without the aid of computers. The Stanford University School Scheduling System provides the foundation for the individualization that is the heart of Marshall's program.

The increased use of such technology in education is both desirable and inevitable. The danger is that our wisdom will not grow to match our new technology. The blending of technology and teaching at Marshall indicates that we can be optimistic about the ability of our schools to utilize technical achievements in the advancement of education.

Melvin W. Barnes, Superintendent
Portland Public Schools
Portland, Oregon

Preface

Marshall High School has pioneered a system of educational reform. The philosophies undergirding the system are not unique to Marshall High School. They are applicable to all secondary schools that dare to break the "traditional rules and regulations," the lockstep of curriculum and classroom. Marshall's innovations merit consideration by all schools in which there is dissatisfaction with the *status quo*—with the amount of individualization—and with problems of staff use and the extent of pupil responsibility now possible.

In the same way that the innovations at Marshall High School have been a result of a team effort of the entire faculty, staff, administration, and students, the book too represents the cooperation of many persons involved in the program at Marshall High School. This in itself is exciting because Marshall was able to achieve as a cooperative venture a level of quality and excellence that would have been impossible for one person, however dedicated or able.

This volume is designed for teachers, administrators, parents, and the general public—for all who are interested in the report of a successful and substantial educational experiment. Professional educators will find many answers to their respective trouble areas. Parents will receive an insight to educational philosophy coupled with a better understanding of the school and its relation to the student, family, and community. The general public will recognize the pressing need for alteration.

Computerization, modular-flexible scheduling, team teaching, independent study, and all the other phases referred to in these pages are certainly not set forth as a panacea. Solutions to problems which are the result of generations are never immediate. What is important is that a first step has been taken. The fact that new approaches inevitably initiate new problems should not minimize the effectiveness and success of this program.

The educational goals of Marshall High School include helping a student think for himself. He must criticize, evaluate, and identify himself in relation to his environment. The program and structure of Marshall High School enhances that opportunity. This is true because the flexible structure and organization of Marshall High School allows this to take place, where more rigid programs do not. Large-group instruction, small-group instruction, open laboratories, independent study, and completely unscheduled time as a part of the student's individual curriculum make this possible. But the structure of a program means nothing without the sensitive participation of the staff. The structure does not *cause* a good program; it *allows* a good program to succeed and encourages creative staff efforts.

Concern is a major prerequisite for the administrator who decides to undertake innovation. He must be concerned with the basic educational philosophy of his school, concerned for the community which his school serves, concerned for the welfare of society as a whole, and most important, he must be concerned for the student as an individual. Our democracy has grown, and with advancement has come the industrialization and technicalization of almost all phases of our environment. Mass production and efficiency have become watchwords which have been difficult to translate into sensitive educational programs. Schools have felt this surge of technology and have been caught in the waves of centralization, consolidation, and in most cases, impersonalization. The need to identify the individual as the essential backbone of our democratic structure has become exceptionally apparent. We must devise programs which exploit technology and not the individual in a technological society. All who have been involved in the development of the Marshall program have attempted to keep this principle as a requisite for all educational decisions. Machines must serve us, not control our educational decisions.

In the new design, the student is most important! The entire program is constructed with this thought in mind. The idea is to identify each and every student. Lectures, impersonal but necessary, can be given to 100 or 200 with equal effectiveness; but the balance comes with individual conferences and small groups, made possible by the use of the large-group presentations. These latter phases allow the individuality of students to surface. Here the student speaks, questions, discusses, and criticizes. Through independent study the pupil learns responsibility, for he must choose how to use his unscheduled time. The resources and opportunities are there; the choice of pursuit lies within the individual. For the first time since the "Little Red Schoolhouse," education may have found a way to base its program on individual needs. The belief in the individual is not new. But the means to implement this belief is new.

When educational offerings are individualized for students' needs and desires and when the program is designed in the light of the abilities and desires of the professional staff administering the program, the curriculum in its entirety must reflect a plan peculiar to that school. Computerization makes possible a framework sufficiently flexible to honor individualistic, personal considerations as well as subject-area peculiarities. In Marshall High School, that which was considered suitable was adopted; that which was not considered suitable was discarded. Such is flexible education. There is still a gap between what we know and what we can do. Compromises have been required and will continue to be needed, but the gap is getting smaller and smaller at Marshall.

Dr. Petrequin's decision to step bravely into innovation required a boldness deserving emulation in all schools seeking to find new levels of quality. The success that Marshall High School has experienced cannot be attributed to new machines or systems but to a staff not afraid to use them.

Dwight W. Allen
Dean, School of Education
University of Massachusetts
Amherst, Massachusetts

Contents

List of Contributors

James R. Barchek
Instructor in English, University of Oregon, Eugene, Oregon. Formerly English Department Chairman, Marshall High School

Rose B. Coffman
Administrative Vice-principal, Marshall High School

Gary Cummings
Teacher, English Department, Marshall High School

Kay Elliott
Director, In-service for Innovation, the Oregon Compact, Portland High School Project. Formerly Chairman, Ninth-grade English–Social Studies Department, Marshall High School

William R. Gray, Jr.
Principal, Washington High School, Portland, Oregon. Formerly Vice-principal, Curriculum and Instruction, Marshall High School

David S. Mesirow
Teacher, Social Studies Department, Marshall High School

Lyle K. Meyer
Chairman, English Department, Marshall High School

William H. Oberteuffer
Chairman, Science Department, Jackson High School, Portland, Oregon. Formerly Chairman, Science Department, Marshall High School

Gaynor Petrequin
Principal, Marshall High School. Instructor, School of Education, University of Portland. Director, Portland Center, Pepperdine College Department of Continuing Education

William G. Tapfer
Vice-principal, Curriculum and Instruction, and Project Director, Marshall High School

Individualizing Learning through Modular-Flexible Programming

1

A Computer-Generated, Teacher-Developed, Modular-Flexible Schedule

Gaynor Petrequin and William G. Tapfer

The existing Marshall program was conceived by the Marshall staff as a means of utilizing teacher and student time more effectively than is possible in a traditional program. The major goal is to individualize teaching and learning through the use of a variety of techniques. It involves breaking the school day into small segments (modules) of time so that class sessions might be more closely constructed in length of time and number of meetings in order to fit the activity taking place within the classroom and the characteristics of the students comprising the particular section. Allowances are also made for variations in group size of from six to four hundred students.

About 80 percent of the Marshall staff is organized into approximately forty teaching teams. The four teaching-learning modes utilized are large-group instruction, medium-size groups for laboratory activities, small-group learning experiences, and independent study. The schedule of each student allows for considerable independent study, which is the most valuable time for most students in terms of individualized learning.

ORGANIZING THE PROGRAM

During the school year 1961–1962, a number of exploratory team-teaching situations developed as the result of the experimental attitude which prevailed in the school. Each team consisted of two or three instructors, usually a student teacher, and sometimes the developmental reading teacher. Experimentation during this year led to establishment of additional teams in 1962–1963. During this year, the entire staff was involved in experimentation and in investigation of the possibilities and potential of modular-flexible scheduling. Consultative services were supplied by the School of Education at Stanford University and by other nationally recognized authorities in staff utilization.

In the winter of 1962–1963, a tentative plan was devised and presented to a large Marshall faculty committee including all department chairmen. Their decision to support the revolutionary type of experiment implied was enthusiastic. From the recommendations of this committee, a final plan was prepared and approved by officials of the Portland public schools. Funds were requested under the *Oregon Program.* Oregon Program funds originated from the Ford Foundation and were specified for improving teacher education and for stimulating the assimilation into classrooms of new teaching techniques, new teaching technology, new plans of organization, and new ways of utilizing professional educators, interns, and aides. This cooperative program to improve education involved the state department of education, Oregon colleges and universities, and local school districts in the state. A grant of $60,000 was approved for Marshall High School for the first year to cover anticipated additional cost of the pioneering venture, particularly for in-service education of staff, coordination, and instructional assistance for teachers. The Portland School District made a substantial contribution in terms of administrative services, redeployed staff time, facilities, and materials.

The invitation of Dr. Dwight W. Allen, associate professor of education at Stanford University, to join with the secondary education project at Stanford in producing and implementing a computerized modular-flexible schedule with the aid of the

IBM 7090 computer was accepted by Dr. Gaynor Petrequin, principal of Marshall High School. The proposal—jointly developed by Dr. Petrequin, Roy Carlson, project director, and the district's administrative leaders—called for the administration and faculty of John Marshall High School to develop a program to better meet the educational needs of all students through (1) improving the use of time with increased attention to pupil variables, subject variables, and the talents and training of teachers; (2) combining the benefits of many small experimental programs in widespread parts of the country with some unique ideas developed at Marshall to test the applicability of flexible programming and team teaching to a large urban high school; (3) providing educators in Oregon and the Northwest with a demonstration of administrative and teaching arrangements from which they might derive benefit.

In the spring of the 1962–1963 school year, the staff of each department at Marshall High School was asked the basic question, "How would you like to teach your course next year without the limitations of a conventional schedule?" From the answers given, course structures, teacher team assignments, and room utilization needs were projected. The faculty members were encouraged to think in terms of large- and small-group instruction and various forms of laboratory groups, together with independent study for all students. From the teacher recommendations, the decision was made to divide the school day into 21 twenty-minute modules, or periods of time. Thus, a large-group presentation might be two modules, or forty minutes, less four minutes passing time; and a lab meeting might be as long as five modules, or 100 minutes. Any multiple of these short time blocks could be requested in order to satisfy the needs of the students and of the particular activity taking place in the course. Figure 1–1 illustrates this concept. The faculty also recommended extending the school day by forty minutes to provide more flexibility in the school program.

Following several months of planning course structures, teacher assignments, and room utilization needs, basic input data were submitted to the Stanford Project. After four years of experimentation and the expenditure of considerable resources, Stan-

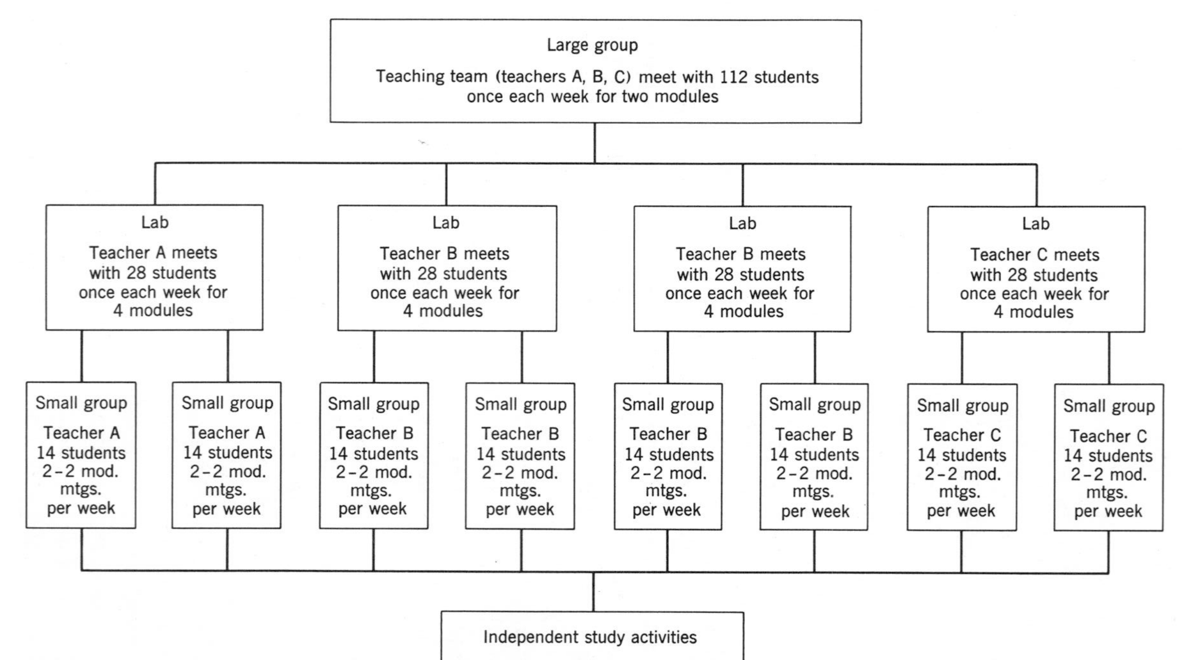

FIGURE 1-1. Variable course structure concept chart

ford produced the first computer-generated school program in August, 1963, for Marshall High School.

Because of the pioneering nature of the project, many critical problems were encountered during this first year. The machine process was successful in scheduling all variables that were anticipated; however, there was considerable need for improvising by the faculty in order to put the program into operation in September, 1963. At any rate, a great forward step had been taken. The "lockstep" and "eggcrate" format of secondary education was decisively broken, and the possibility of implementing new methods of teaching and learning was provided.

IN-SERVICE TRAINING

In addition to the experimentation that took place by certain teachers or teams of teachers during the year prior to implementing the new design, many Marshall staff members attended a two-week Oregon Program workshop. This workshop was designed to acquaint Oregon educators with the general need for educational improvement and with possible innovations in staff organization and teaching techniques which might provide such improvement. In the summer of 1963, the Oregon Program sponsored a secondary team-teaching workshop which was conducted through the cooperative efforts of the state department of education and the Portland public schools. This workshop, held at Marshall and Wilson High Schools in Portland, permitted a number of Marshall teachers to participate. Emphasis was placed on both the theory and practice of team teaching; and from this combined summer high school and teacher workshop came reactions from students and teachers, indications of building needs, and experience in the use of paraprofessionals. As an in-service activity to affect teacher attitudes and behavior, this workshop was phenomenally successful.

Prior to the start of the 1963–1964 school year, all department chairmen and some teaching-team leaders participated in a local ten-day workshop. The entire faculty at Marshall returned to the school two days early for a general workshop in techniques of large-group presentation, small-group activities, and independent study. In succeeding years teacher committees actively engaged in experimentation and exploration of these relatively new teaching modes. These experienced teachers then became "experts" in the field and, at the beginning of each school year, helped the Marshall administrators train teachers who were new to the staff.

MODIFICATION OF FACILITIES

The Marshall program provides for resource centers, team planning areas, individual study spaces for students, office space for teachers, and a student union area to be used by students for relaxation. Since the school building was relatively new and of modern design, it had such features as conference rooms, combined rooms with folding doors, and a small auditorium seating 400 which was adaptable for large-group presentations. Since the inception of the new program, building modifications have been made to provide teacher office space. Five standard-size classrooms were each divided in half to provide ten smaller rooms for use by small groups. Also, two walls were removed to provide adequate resource-center space. A few other minor building changes were made.

THEORY INTO PRACTICE

Under the new design, the basic time framework was changed from a conventional seven-period day of fifty-five minutes per period to a twenty-minute modular schedule consisting of 21 modules per day, or 105 modules per weekly cycle. Each school day begins with an eleven-minute registration period during which an attendance check is made, daily announcements are read, and teachers have an opportunity to work with individuals in the registration room regarding their academic progress. The first module of the school day following the registration period begins at 8:20 A.M., and dismissal time is 3:15 P.M. All students are required to remain on the campus during the school day unless early dismissal has been granted for a specific reason or they need to do off-campus research. Originally the program included a one-hour block of time on Friday mornings for school activities such as assemblies and class meetings. This had the advantage of not encroaching on class time for any of these activities. After three years, however, it was felt that students wanted an alternate time schedule in order to schedule assemblies any day of the week. This was done by eliminating two minutes from each module on assembly days and has proved to be quite satisfactory. It allows for more flexibility during the school week for the variety of special activities that take place. Lunchtime consists of any two consecutive modules from module 10 to 16. This is not on an assigned basis; students may eat at any time within this block that they have unstructured time. Occasionally a student may have only one module for lunch in order to avoid a conflict in an otherwise satisfactory schedule. This has not been considered a hardship by students.

As is customary in a secondary school, each student preregisters in the spring for his program of studies for the following year. The program of modular scheduling allows for extensive orientation so that students can make intelligent choices. This involves contact with each of the "feeder" elementary schools, parent and student visits, school-newspaper description of courses, open classes for direct observation by students, student-parent worksheets, and most importantly, individual conferencing of each student with his counselor within a ten-day period of time.

It would be physically impossible to manually prepare a master program with the complexity of the design used at Marshall or to assign the entire student body by hand to individual class sections; therefore, this function continues to be performed at Stanford University using the IBM 7090 computer. Although the computer is necessary to generate the master schedule and load students into the schedule, it is necessary later to make some manual adjustments for certain individual students and to hand-schedule students new to the school.

A better understanding of the individual student's schedule can be gained by a study of the student program of Mary Jones, a junior, and of John Smith, a freshman, Figures 1–2 and 1–3. These schedules would be considered typical for most Marshall students, although it would be difficult to locate two identical

Reg. room ________

Student Program
John Marshall High School
3905 S.E. 91st Avenue
Portland, Oregon 97266

Name Jones Mary
Last First

Counselor ________________

Sex M (F) Year in school 9 10 (11) 12

B schedule starting time	Module	A schedule starting time	Monday			Tuesday			Wednesday			Thursday			Friday		
8:05	Reg.	8:05	Course	Rm	Teacher	Course	Rm	Teacher	Course	Rm	Teacher	Course	Rm	Teacher	Course	Rm	Teacher
9:01	1	8:20	H5-6 Lab	A25	Robin.							SB1-2 Lab	C17	Voit			
9:19	2	8:40	"	"	"				G3-4 Lab	C32	Neelan	"	"	"	G3-4 Lab	C32	Neelan
9:37	3	9:00	"	"	"				"	"	"	"	"	"	"	"	"
9:55	4	9:20	"	"	"							"	"	"			
10:13	5	9:40							E5-6B Lab	B47	Lane	"	"	"	E5-6B Lab	B47	Lane
10:31	6	10:00	SB1-2 SG	C17	Voit				"	"	"				"	"	"
10:49	7	10:20	"	"	"	G3-4 LG	C32	Sager	"	"	"				"	"	"
11:07	8	10:40				"	"	"									
11:25	9	11:00															
11:43	10	11:20	G3-4 MG	C33	Sager	Lunch			G3-4 MG	C33	Sager	G3-4 MG	C33	Sager	G3-4 MG	C33	Sager
12:01	11	11:40	"	"	"	Lunch			"	"	"	"	"	"	"	"	"
12:19	12	12:00	E5-6B SG	B44	Lane	SB1-2 LG	B67	Tsuboi	H5-6 LG	B67	Robin.	SB1-2 LG	B67	Tsuboi	Lunch		
12:37	13	12:20	"	"	"	"	"	"	"	"	"	"	"	"	Lunch		
12:55	14	12:40	Lunch						Lunch			Lunch			E5-6B LG	B67	Team
1:13	15	1:00	Lunch						Lunch			Lunch			"	"	"
1:31	16	1:20				SS5-6 SG	B28	Simpson	SS5-6 SG	B28	Simpson	SS5-6 SG	B28	Simpson			
1:49	17	1:40				"	"	"	"	"	"	"	"	"			
2:07	18	2:00													H5-6 SG	A25	Robin.
2:25	19	2:20													"	"	"
2:43	20	2:40							SS5-6 LG	B67	Sturd.				SS5-6 LG	B67	Sturd.
3:01	21	3:00							"	"	"				"	"	"

3:15 Dismissal

FIGURE 1-2

Student Program
John Marshall High School
3905 S.E. 91st Avenue
Portland, Oregon 97266

Reg. room ________

Counselor ________________

Name Smith (Last) John (First)

Sex (M) F   Year in school (9) 10 11 12

B schedule starting time	Module	A schedule starting time	Monday			Tuesday			Wednesday			Thursday			Friday		
8:05	Reg.	8:05	Course	Rm	Teacher	Course	Rm	Teacher	Course	Rm	Teacher	Course	Rm	Teacher	Course	Rm	Teacher
9:01	1	8:20	IA1-2 LG	B67	Team	IA1-2 Lab	A28	Balzer				IA1-2 Lab	A28	Balzer			
9:19	2	8:40	"	"	"	"	"	"	MuB5-8	B57	Salyard	"	"	"	MuB5-8	B57	Salyard
9:37	3	9:00				"	"	"	"	"	"	"	"	"	"	"	"
9:55	4	9:20				"	"	"	"	"	"	"	"	"	"	"	"
10:13	5	9:40				E1-2 Lab	B8	Fiser									
10:31	6	10:00				"	"	"	PE1-2 Lab	Gym	Chris.				PE1-2 Lab	Gym	Chris.
10:49	7	10:20				"	"	"	"	"	"				"	"	"
11:07	8	10:40							"	"	"				"	"	"
11:25	9	11:00							"	"	"				"	"	"
11:43	10	11:20				SS1-2 SG	B27B	Lindsay	Lunch			SS1-2 SG	B27B	Lindsay	IA1-2 IL	A28	Balzer
12:01	11	11:40	Lunch			"	"	"	Lunch			"	"	"	"	"	"
12:19	12	12:00	Lunch			PE1-2 Lab	Gym	Chris.				Lunch			Lunch		
12:37	13	12:20	MuB5-8 HB	B67	Salyard	"	"	"				Lunch			Lunch		
12:55	14	12:40	"	"	"	"	"	"	E1-2 SG	B6	Fiser				E1-2 SG	B6	Fiser
1:13	15	1:00	"	"	"	Lunch			"	"	"				"	"	"
1:31	16	1:20	E1-2 LG	A30	Team	E1-2 LG	A30	Team	SS1-2 Lab	B67	Lindsay						
1:49	17	1:40	"	"	"	"	"	"	"	"	"						
2:07	18	2:00				"	"	"	"	"	"						
2:25	19	2:20	MA1-2 MG	C55	Schmid	MuB5-8	B67	Salyard	MA1-2 MG	C55	Schmid	MA1-2 MG	C55	Schmid	MA1-2 MG	C55	Schmid
2:43	20	2:40	"	"	"	"	"	"	"	"	"	"	"	"	"	"	"
3:01	21	3:00	"	"	"	"	"	"	"	"	"	"	"	"	"	"	"

3:15 Dismissal

FIGURE 1-3

schedules. Mary Jones, an average student, consulted with her counselor in February or March and then preregistered for Junior English, American History, second-year German, Biology, and third-year Home Economics. In each course, the structure has been designed by the teacher or teaching team for that subject. As an example, Mary will start her English cycle on Friday with a two-module large group. This large group will involve all students of average ability taking Junior English (approximately 300). On Monday she will meet with a small group numbering between 6 and 15 students. On Wednesday and Friday she has a three-module English lab (30 to 60 students) devoted to skill-building activities. Mary has the same teacher for all phases of her English course with the exception of the large group, which has a team of two teachers. Mary Jones has forty modules of unstructured time during the week which she may use in any or all of the following ways:

Work in an open lab (home economics, foreign language, biology)
Study in the library
Study in a resource center (seven available)
Conference with her teachers or counselor
Relax in the student union
Participate in a prerogative (noncredit, enrichment) course
Pursue independent-study project (possibly off campus)
Visit interesting classes (large and small groups)
Serve the school in the capacity of teacher assistant or assistant to a resource-center aide

John Smith is a freshman boy and has more structure during the week than Mary Jones. His program consists of twenty-seven modules of unstructured time and is typical of the amount of independent-study time given to freshmen. This program also allows for individual responsibility and decision making on the part of the student, but to a lesser degree than upper-division students.

The teaching assignment and load of each teacher is determined in the spring for the following year. A typical teacher would be involved in class activity for approximately two-thirds of his teaching time. The one-third unstructured time would be devoted primarily to student conferencing, planning, and evaluating student work. If the teacher is a part of a teaching team, a common time (one hour per week) will be designated on his program when all members of that team are able to meet together for planning purposes. Also, each teacher is responsible for about forty minutes of supervision during each week in the student union.

The department chairman has a reduced teaching load, depending upon the size of his department. Lyle Meyer, English department chairman, is responsible for seventeen teachers and has about one-third of his time structured for teaching purposes. The department chairman acts as supervisor to the teachers in his department, meets in a group of department chairmen with the vice-principal for curriculum and instruction and the principal to confer on basic school policies and procedures, has responsibility for his resource center, and supervises clerks and aides within the department. Figures 1–4 and 1–5 detail the program of a teacher and department chairman.

Most teachers involved in a modular-flexible program do not have a single room of their own but rather meet their classes in rooms that are more suitable for the particular learning mode. As an example, a teacher will meet a large group in a room seating a maximum of 400 students. His small-group meetings will be in seminar rooms and medium-size groups in standard lab rooms. This means that most rooms are used by two or more teachers; consequently, the teaching staff must now be provided with office space. At Marshall High School this space was found in many different areas. Small conference rooms are used for this purpose. Some cubicles were constructed, and in one instance, a carpet was laid on the floor of a large custodial storeroom in order to provide adequate facilities for teacher offices. Wherever possible the teacher offices have been located adjacent to resource centers so that teachers and students will have ready access to each other.

Reg. room ______

Teachers' Program
John Marshall High School
3905 S.E. 91st Avenue
Portland, Oregon 97266

Name Meyer (Last) Lyle (First)

Department English

B schedule starting time	Module	A schedule starting time	Monday			Tuesday			Wednesday			Thursday			Friday		
			Course	Rm	Teacher	Course	Rm	Teacher	Course	Rm	Teacher	Course	Rm	Teacher	Course	Rm	Teacher
8:05	Reg.	8:05															
9:01	1	8:20	E5-6A LG	B48		E5-6A LG	B48		Extended	Reg.	Room	E5-6A Lab	B24		Extended	Reg.	Room
9:19	2	8:40	"	"		"	"		Student conference			"	"		Dep't. supervision		
9:37	3	9:00	Dep't. supervision			E5-6A Team planning			"	"		"	"		"	"	
9:55	4	9:20	"	"		"			E7-8B Lab	B26		"	"		"	"	
10:13	5	9:40	"	"		E7-8B LG	B67		"	"		Student conference			"	"	
10:31	6	10:00	Intern conference			"	"		"	"		E7-8B Lab	B49		E5-6A SG	A13	
10:49	7	10:20	"	"		E5-6A SG	B38		"	"		"	"		"	"	
11:07	8	10:40	"	"		"	"		Student conference			Planning			E5-6A SG	B38	
11:25	9	11:00	Student conference			"	"		"	"		"			"	"	
11:43	10	11:20	"	"		E3-4EE Lab	B 6		"	"		"			Lunch		
12:01	11	11:40	"	"		"	"		"	"		"			"		
12:19	12	12:00	E3-4EE SG	B 6		Lunch			E3-4EESG	B49		Lunch			E3-4EE SG	B49	
12:37	13	12:20	"	"		"			"	"		Lunch			"	"	
12:55	14	12:40	Lunch			E5-6A Team planning			Lunch			E3-4EE Lab	B38		Student conference		
1:13	15	1:00	Lunch			"			"			"	"		"	"	
1:31	16	1:20	Cafeteria duty			E5-6ASG	B46		Dep't. supervision						"	"	
1:49	17	1:40	"	"		"	"		"	"		E7-8B Team planning			"	"	
2:07	18	2:00	Planning			"	"		"	"		"	"		Planning		
2:25	19	2:20	"			Planning			City dep't. chrm.			"	"		"		
2:43	20	2:40	"			"			meeting			Dep't. supervision			"		
3:01	21	3:00	"			"			"			"	"		"		

3:15 Dismissal

FIGURE 1-4

Reg. room A21

Teachers' Program
John Marshall High School
3905 S.E. 91st Avenue
Portland, Oregon 97266

Name Tunks (Last) Roger (First)

Department Industrial arts

B schedule starting time	Module	A schedule starting time	Monday			Tuesday			Wednesday			Thursday			Friday		
			Course	Rm	Teacher	Course	Rm	Teacher	Course	Rm	Teacher	Course	Rm	Teacher	Course	Rm	Teacher
8:05	Reg.	8:05															
9:01	1	8:20	IA1-2 LG	B67		IA1-2 Lab	A26		Extended	Reg.		IA1-2 Lab	A26		Extended	Reg.	
9:19	2	8:40	"			"			IA1-2 Lab	A26		"			IA1-2 Lab	A26	
9:37	3	9:00	Planning			"			"			"			"		
9:55	4	9:20	IE1-2 Lab	A21		"			"			"			"		
10:13	5	9:40	"			Planning			"			Open lab	A21		"		
10:31	6	10:00	"			"			Planning			"			IA3-4 LG	B67	
10:49	7	10:20	"			IE3-4 Lab	A21		"			"			"		
11:07	8	10:40	Open lab	A21		"			IA5-6 LG	B67		"			Planning		
11:25	9	11:00	"			"			"			"			"		
11:43	10	11:20	"			"			Lunch			Lunch			IA1-2 IL	A26	
12:01	11	11:40	"			Lunch			Lunch			Lunch			"		
12:19	12	12:00	"			Lunch			Open lab	A21		IE3-4 IL	A21		Lunch		
12:37	13	12:20	Lunch			Student conference			"			"			Lunch		
12:55	14	12:40	Lunch			"	"		"			Student conference			Planning		
1:13	15	1:00	Planning			"	"		"			"	"		"		
1:31	16	1:20	AC1-2 IL	A26		IA1-2 IL	A26		AC1-2 IL	A26		"	"		AC1-2 IL	A26	
1:49	17	1:40	"			"			"			IE1-2 IL	A30		"		
2:07	18	2:00	"			IE1-2 Lab	A21		"			"			"		
2:25	19	2:20	Student conference			"			Team planning			Student conference			Student conference		
2:43	20	2:40	"	"		"			" "			Supervision			"	"	
3:01	21	3:00	"	"		"			" "			"			"	"	

3:15 Dismissal

FIGURE 1-5

During the first four years of modular-flexible scheduling at Marshall High School, many changes took place. As would be expected in a program of this complexity, teachers have had considerable opportunity to experiment with how students learn best. They have used the flexibility available to structure their courses in order to more closely meet the needs of the individual. The value of more than one large-group meeting during the week for a single course has been questioned by most teachers, serious consideration has been given to the ideal length of time for small-group meetings, and maximum attention spans have been observed in various activities. The open-laboratory concept seems to be accepted by a growing number of teachers. Perhaps most important, teachers have found that given the opportunity, most students can become responsible to a large degree for their own education. Under the new design, school has become more interesting for teachers and students alike.

The need for continual curriculum assessment and modification is more apparent in this system, since teachers working together in teams are much more prone to question traditional practices as they assess their course objectives in terms of their particular students. As a result, teachers are moving into interdisciplinary curriculum approaches and into the area of *performance curriculum,* in which the criterion of time is replaced with one of performance. Certainly modular-flexible programming cannot be considered a panacea for the education of all students, but in the minds of the Marshall staff it has provided a vehicle to satisfy more closely the needs of each individual in this school.

2

Large-Group Instruction

David S. Mesirow

The large group in a modular-flexible design is generally referred to in a physical sense as a situation requiring more than twenty students to focus their attention on a single source of instructional activity and usually containing from perhaps as few as forty to four hundred or more students. However, the large group is really a state of mind. Its definition, in this sense, is determined by what is expected of the student and the teacher. The ideal of a small group is to provide for a maximum of active student involvement, especially on the verbal level. In the context of large-group instruction, the student is clearly a member of an audience; the situation is *presenter* dominated.[1] The student's role is one of watching, hearing, and noting what happens during the presentation and, it is hoped, reacting cognitively but covertly.

The major assumption and leading pedagogical justification for

[1] The word *presenter* is appropriate because a large group may be conducted by a teacher; a "resource" person; a student; or a group of teachers, students, or others.

this type of grouping is that it serves a number of unique functions.[2] There is a generally shared belief that the large group offers a special format to provide for enrichment and motivational stimulus. Ideally, it is an open-ended presentation of provocative ideas. Students are confronted with material in a form and fashion that they would not otherwise receive. This generally rules out straight lectures, especially those based on books that are read by the students. In another sense, the large group is designed to accomplish an efficient presentation of material that would otherwise be endlessly repeated and less excitingly communicated in the conventional classroom.

There are several elements of the large-group instructional mode that need close examination. The setting of the large group and the equipment involved, the presenter and the presentation, and the audience will be the general features of the large group considered in detail in this chapter.[3]

Before the survey of the large group begins, it is necessary to consider the relationship of this concept of grouping to team teaching. Almost every department at Marshall High School is divided into teams. When flexible scheduling was first instituted, teams were formed on the basis of teachers' major teaching loads. This action brought together teachers of very different personalities and philosophical attitudes about teaching and education. Much time and energy went into the management of the incompatibility. Team planning for the large group during the first year found more time absorbed by philosophical and personality differences among team members than by concrete planning for the course and the large groups. In a few cases, the differences led to severe misunderstandings about the purpose of large groups, resulting in arguments among teachers that tended to affect the morale of the teams. Since the plans of the team provide the profile of the course for the year, as well as the spe-

[2] For example, the freshman program is designed, in part, to introduce students to the functioning of the flexible schedule. Consequently, considerable time is spent in the large group discussing and working with the skills needed by students for the large group.

[3] For a consideration of how the large group operates within the context of a departmental program, the reader should examine Chapters 7 and 8.

cific presentations to be given in the large groups, it cannot be stressed too strongly that it is important for the team to agree on the nature and purpose of the course it seeks to teach.

Though certain deficiencies in large-group presentations during the first year were due in part to the fact that this was a new experience for everyone, a part was also due to the differences of team members. For instance, critiquing of the large-group performance by other team members, which is indispensable for the improvement of presentations, was delayed. Certainly there will always be a "shakedown" period as the teachers on a team adjust to each other. Eventually experience and constructive attitudes result in workable compromises and the development of a team concensus concerning the large group. However, practical experience underscores the suggestion that when a modular-flexible schedule is contemplated, considerable attention should be given to this area of personnel relations well in advance of its implementation.

In terms of planning, one of the first problems that must be dealt with by the team is the coordination of the material presented in the large group with the discussions that occur in small group. In a sense, the large group can serve as the focus of continuity for the course. The exact implications the presentations have for the small groups certainly are decided by the team or by each teacher as he makes his plans for small groups. Too rigid a connection between large and small groups seems to raise questions of creativity and independence. A teacher may come to feel that he is merely a technician, plugging in various items from the large group in a methodical review of what was said and seen. Yet, some continuity is imperative lest the students feel they are taking two different courses in the subject—courses that have little or no relation to each other.

Beyond the problem of continuity, planning involves another consideration. Purpose will determine the form and content of the large group. For instance, should the presentations strive to give a "balanced" interpretation of a problem—outlining various definitions of the problem and the various possible solutions to the problem—or should the presentations be oriented to provocative interpretations that place the responsibility of criticism on the shoulders of the student? How should a science teacher present evolution; a social studies teacher, the entrepreneurs of the late nineteenth century; an English teacher, the meaning of *Hamlet*? Should the presentation provide answers or should it raise questions? Certainly either approach may be used, but the team should clearly understand the intention of the presenter. Otherwise the ensuing consideration of the material in the small group may travel down the path of a character analysis of the presenter rather than an examination of the content that was presented.

A third problem of planning involves the amount a team does in advance of large-group performances. On the one hand, it is desirable to have detailed plans in order to ensure the availability of speakers and audio-visual materials or to allow for the research that will serve as the foundation for a presentation. Another benefit of advanced planning is that students can be notified of the upcoming program, allowing them an opportunity to plan their studies ahead. On the other hand, it is desirable to take advantage of opportunities that occur without advance notice, particularly in the form of outside speakers. As one instance, the senior social studies team was faced with a decision, in its large-group presentations, of continuing a carefully planned examination of automation or of providing for an outspoken candidate for the United States Senate to speak to seniors. Some balance between continuity and flexibility must be struck, and this requires a team to be receptive toward revision and reconsideration of its plans for the large group.

There are no easy or simple formulas for solutions to these three problems; suffice it to warn of their existence.

THE SETTING AND THE EQUIPMENT

Shifting attention to the large group itself, the first items to explore are the equipment and the setting. Certainly large rooms are necessary to accommodate the numbers of a typical large group. At Marshall High School the center for large-group presentations is the auditorium. This room is equipped with a lectern console containing a microphone, tape recorder, and record player. At the presenter's right is an overhead projector. On stage is an electrically controlled screen, and in the rear of the auditorium is a projection booth containing a permanently mounted motion-picture projector. At present, the only suitable location for a slide projector is in the audience. One immediate improvement of the situation would be to centralize all controls within the auditorium at the lectern console. As of now, the lights, the screen, the curtains, and the slide projector can be controlled only at points quite distant from the presenter and by some other person. In another large-group room, there is a console, designed by one of the teachers in the school, which permits the presenter to control everything from one location.

The equipment for large-group presentations is, unfortunately, not sufficiently emphasized in the literature concerning modular-flexible scheduling. A very high degree of coordination between teachers and those in charge of audio-visual equipment is imperative. Without such coordination, a teacher suddenly can be confronted with the horror of handling a large group for which the equipment and/or the operator has not arrived. The coordination of the equipment falls into two areas, the process of obtaining the desired equipment and the operation of the equipment itself. The burden of responsibility for coordination of the former should and does fall upon the presenter. Only he knows the equipment he needs. The school, in turn, must provide a smooth-running system for obtaining equipment and operators. During the first three years of the modular program, an audio-visual center was utilized in which most of the available equipment was stored and which handled the assignment of operators. Orders were placed in advance so that ample time was provided to fill the needs of the various departments. However, the center did become overburdened from time to time by the demands placed upon it. A plan was developed and implemented during the fourth year of the program whereby most of the equipment was decentralized to the various departmental resource centers after each of the three large-group rooms had been equipped with permanently located equipment. A full-time audio-visual clerk is now employed whose sole job is the efficient management of the school's entire audio-visual needs.

A further consideration of the setting of the large group involves the positioning of the audience. Certainly the size of the large group is determined by the size of the room available. Also, the type of seating arrangement is determined by the space available. Several methods of seating have been tried. Students have been placed alphabetically in alternate seats, or next to one another, or sometimes by their small-group section. In senior social studies and English, it was found that students, generally, were hostile to alternate seats. They felt it implied a lack of maturity on their part, and they were quite resentful. After the first year, the practice in these courses has been to seat the students differently. A frequent arrangement has been to seat the students together in small-group sections—all the small groups of each teacher sit in a specific section of the large-group room. In any case, the students are assigned to numbered seats, and roll is taken by noting the numbers on the empty seats. Attendance may then be taken by a teacher, an aide, or even a student.

Whatever discipline problems have resulted in large groups, and they have been very few, have been resolved either by removing the student from the room or by moving the student to an isolated area where close supervision may be given. The occasional need for supervision illustrates the desirability of having most members of the teaching team present during a large-group presentation. The presenter may continue while any disturbance is handled by a colleague. It may be advisable to have the team present to ensure continuity between large and small groups, but even more important, the presence of other teachers clearly contributes to a positive learning atmosphere. The critiquing of the presentation, which should occur after most large groups, would of course be difficult without the involvement of the entire team.

THE PRESENTER AND THE PRESENTATION

The major reference source for the strategy and tactics of large-group presentations should be the biography of a circus ringmaster. There is a premium on capturing and sustaining the interest of the audience. Certainly, this demand is made of the teacher in a traditional classroom. However, it becomes a priority item in the large group of our new instructional design. Variety and suspense are the two major attention-attracting devices a presenter should be prepared to use.

The large group is a sight and sound phenomenon, and usually the presenter must be prepared to show as well as talk. The key is, and should be, gaining the attention of the students. Without this, any lesson or idea is lost. This does not mean that one simply panders to students, but it does mean that teachers must continually probe their talents for creativity while developing their presentations.

Most of the teams have found that a forty-minute block of time is sufficient and efficient for a large group. One must always reckon with a student's attention span. There is no question that an exciting program can sustain attention for a considerable time. However, it appears to be impossible to plan "spectaculars" once or twice a week, especially during the first few years of the program. The time and energy that go into planning a "spectacular" large group are incalculable. Depending on the course and the material being presented and the kinds of audio-visual material that are available, the desired time for planning may run from a day to a month. A teacher accumulates presentations as the years go by, and certain strains of preparation are reduced. Still, the presentations of the past require polishing, and this is done with time-consuming special care in the hope that each touch will facilitate communication with the students.

If you are lucky, you have the module before the large group free to prepare last-minute touches or to fuss impatiently for the bell to ring so that the performance may start. Otherwise you arrive, somewhat breathlessly, with an armload of transparencies and with fingers crossed that the equipment is in operating order and is correctly placed. You maneuver through the throng of students making their way to their seats.

"Today" (or the variations, "This morning," "Now," etc.) booms from the loudspeakers, a pause to gain the attention of the audience, and you are under way. Your gaze takes in an audience that has assumed an amazing variety of postures, from the bright-eyed, bushy-tailed to the nodding drowsiness of a student who has had to work late the night before.

Immediately two sources of tension begin to press on your presentation: the pressure of the clock and the coordination of your visual material with what you are saying. The voice—depending upon the presenter, sometimes varied in tone and emphasis or, unfortunately, droning—goes through the prepared material and comes to a close approximately with the end of the module. Once again there are waves of students, this time spilling out into the hall. Some students come forward to raise a question or to argue a point with you. You find yourself answering in all too hurried a fashion as you move up the aisle on your way to a small group. A team member approaches to praise your latest effort—but any extended comment must wait until you both have some unstructured time. You are left with the hope that the next small group may give some inkling of student reaction during the large group. Will your own hopes or fears about the presentation be confirmed?

In the first few years of the Marshall experience, many teachers, particularly in the social studies and English, shifted the material and the format of their presentations from a text-centered, descriptive lecture to an interpretation of the subject being considered, outlining the sources that the students should investigate to criticize the presentation. In other subjects the large group is a place for demonstration and a study of technique. This is true of mathematics, science, industrial arts, and home economics. In all subjects the large group is used for testing.

A presentation may follow one of two general approaches. It can be aimed for a certain group within the audience or it can be designed along the line of a "shotgun blast" by which the presenter hopes to reach every intellectual level in the audience during the course of the presentation. Obviously the latter approach is the most desirable.

Closely related to the approach of a presentation is the amount of material that can be comfortably handled by the presenter and the students. It is almost impossible to determine hard-and-fast suggestions about the quantity of items that should appear in a presentation. The amount will, of course, depend upon the presenter's purpose. However, experience has convinced most teachers of three operating principles. First, it is desirable to have a surplus of material just in case time remains. Second, the number of ideas or concepts to be presented should be very few, perhaps only one or two. And last, any idea must be approached with several examples. Through the use of the overhead projector and with the help of a creative graphic artist, transparencies can be prepared to visually develop and communicate almost any idea.

The typical setting of the large group, the auditorium, contributes to the dramatization of the subject. The effect can be startling, particularly if the presenter calls upon the mechanical aides at his disposal. The more of these devices that can be employed, the greater the possibility is for creating variety and suspense. A dramatic parting of the curtain to reveal a staged situation, the interjection of sound through the record player or the tape recorder, or the projection of a compelling picture on the screen by a film slide can captivate the students. However, the presenter has to be alert to the subtle comparisons that are always present in the student's mind. The presentation, because of its theatrical setting, usually compares unfavorably with the polish and drama of television programs, movies, and stage plays. This is especially true when, for one reason or another, the mechanical equipment sets out to defy the presenter. Contingency planning for such a situation is imperative. Rule one for presenters is to expect an emergency and have a substitute presentation ready at all times.

If students know the presenter, he is challenged to constantly vary his presentations to keep audience interest. An outside presenter—a resource person—may not have to use any of the equipment that is available, for the students are intrigued by unknown people. This is especially true when the subject of the presentation is a matter of deep concern to them. A college student who had been in the South during the summer of 1964 held a senior social studies large group spellbound, past the dismissal time, as he considered the question of prejudice. At times, though, the students have found outside people somewhat trying. Certainly it is true that good speakers have few problems, whereas poor ones have many.

Clearly, some teachers have a flair for this type of teaching performance; others do not. Two options are open to teaching teams. One is to develop in their midst a large-group presenter and make him responsible for preparing most of the presentations. To provide time for research and assembling of material, this teacher's small-group or laboratory load is reduced. The second alternative is to divide large-group presentations among the team members on the basis of special interest and competency in the unit under consideration. The latter tends to divide the responsibility for large group equally among the team members. Marshall has tended, distinctly, in the second direction. There are advantages and disadvantages to both styles. There is a feeling current that the establishment of one presenter would be detrimental to team morale, for it may set up invidious comparisons of teachers by students. Further, it is felt that the large-group presenter would be operating in a vacuum because his direct contact with students would be considerably reduced. Another pressure against specialization is the feeling of being utterly swamped by the responsibility and the work of preparing all the large-group performances for a year. Moreover, students appear to prefer the variety introduced when all members of the team share the large-group responsibilities. It must be recognized, though, that sharing large-group presentations equally tends to make critiquing tender- rather than tough-minded, and that presentations may wind up poorly planned and executed because there is insufficient time to prepare them adequately. However, despite the criticism that may be advanced against the idea of equal responsibility, experience at Marshall would suggest that it creates an air of collective responsibility for the large group and that the desire to improve large-group presentations pervades every member of the team.

Finally, for purposes of variety and interest, students have been directly involved in large-group presentations. Through panels, debates, sociodramas, and speeches, many students have participated in large-group performances. An example of this was a symposium on the question "Are You Free?" conducted by the advanced speech class for the freshmen. In senior social studies, students took the role of senators of the commerce committee, and after considerable study and preparation, successfully portrayed a segment of the hearings on automobile safety for the other members of the senior class in the large group. As with other large groups, great care must be taken in planning and preparation to ensure the interest of the audience.

THE AUDIENCE AND THE EFFECT OF THE LARGE GROUP

Turning to the audience for a consideration of the effect of the large group, it must be admitted that as yet the standards of measurement are crude. Three measures of the large-group effectiveness might be the student's performance on tests, his participation in small group, and his retention of ideas and information, for instance, in his notes. A student's willingness to attend large group or to stay awake are other, informal, measures. Perhaps the best assessment is the observation of students' physical attentiveness. This attending behavior can be assessed by the presenter as well as his teammates in the audience. Isolated student and adult comment about large group is sometimes unreliable. In fact, there may be a curious inverse effect: The more compliments the presenter receives from the adults in the audience, the more he should be prepared for negative reactions from the students. This is generally true at the outset of team teaching because adults tend to use their personal reactions and frames of reference as the basis for their comments rather than their observations of student reaction. Moreover, after any presentation, it seems one student can be found to say that it was the best large group he has ever attended, and another will comment that it was the worst. Most of the favorable comments students make about large group seem to come when the subject or the presenter is "controversial" and the situation has developed emotional overtones. Such an atmosphere usually results when the students are permitted to ask questions of the presenter. Inevitably these situations occur most frequently when the presenter is an outside "resource" person. On occasion, those parents who take a sustained interest in the school will comment about large group. Their statements will cluster around the idea, which they find desirable, that their children are exposed to the thinking and talent of several teachers in the same subject area. Again, none of these measures is precise. However, the general ferment throughout the United States concerning the adequacy of methods for evaluating students holds promise for devising measures of the effect of large-group presentations.

PROSPECTS FOR THE FUTURE

The most immediate improvement in large-group presentations at Marshall can be made by improved equipment. A teaching console with controls centralized at the lectern is needed in the auditorium. The audio-visual equipment is not of the highest quality and too often does not operate satisfactorily. Our experience would indicate that because of continuous use, only the highest-quality equipment should be provided for the large-group rooms. Moreover, a well-trained full-time adult is needed to maintain the audio-visual program with its variety and quantity of equipment and with the requisite number of student operators.

A frequent criticism of educational institutions is the evidence of apparently unnecessary repetition in different departments of the same material. For instance, a student enrolled in social studies, business education, and consumer math may be asked to consider the nature of capital investment or the operation of the price system in the American economy. Or a student enrolled in English and social studies may be asked to examine the question of perception. It would be highly desirable to have the consideration of such questions coordinated among departments, with each bringing its special expertise to bear on the questions. Clearly, the lines that separate departments and their areas of concern are merely arbitrary ones. In the fourth year of the new design, an interdisciplinary course uniting industrial education and English was attempted. During the fifth year, this course was expanded to include English, mathematics, and science, centered on power mechanics as the "core." This course for non-college-bound boys is a good example of the integration of four separate areas of the school curriculum. Also, the fifth year saw the implementation of a very fine humanities course involving a true integration of literature, art, and music. These developments raise concrete hopes for new dimensions in teaching and learning.

Further, a desirable outcome of the schedule has been the increased willingness of teachers to cross department lines to participate in large-group presentations. Several teachers have volunteered to be "guest" presenters. The director of the distributive-education program presented an examination of job opportunity and outlook to a senior social studies large group during a consideration of the American economy. An American history teacher was asked to provide the historical background for an English large group studying *The Diary of Anne Frank.* A senior social studies teacher was asked to speak to a freshman large group on the foreign policy of the Soviet Union. There are many such examples, indicating a marked improvement in staff utilization.

Another outcome of the new scheduling design has been the opportunity for students from any grade level to visit various large groups during their unstructured time. Through the use of a special-announcement bulletin board in the main hall, particularly interesting large-group presentations are advertised and noted by the students. This voluntary auditing of large groups, and also interestingly of the small groups, is a growing development not originally foreseen.

Undoubtedly there are a variety of other activities for large-group presentations which we have not yet uncovered or have not yet utilized. Video-tape productions are well suited to the large group. Present plans call for the purchase of video-tape equipment. This will be particularly helpful as additional supporting instructional technology for use in the large group.

CONCLUSION

This chapter has been devoted to exploring the dimensions of the large group. Most features of this kind of grouping concern the state of mind of both the teacher and the student. Clearly, an obligation has been placed on both, constantly, to reconsider their attitudes about teaching and being taught.

Those teachers who have experimented with new thoughts in curriculum and new teaching strategies have found themselves involved in a pioneering adventure. The scale of operation that may be mounted in a large group (in terms of numbers, equipment, and setting) has not been previously available to the classroom teacher. And as this chapter suggests, such an adventure is a scary, frustrating, challenging, and fulfilling experience.

3

Small-Group Learning

Kay Elliott

As with other innovative practices at Marshall High School, small-group instruction has been an exploration of the uncharted area between theories advanced by educational leaders and reality. Teachers have examined, reexamined, accepted, rejected, and experimented with ideas proposed in previous workshop experiences and through association with the leading proponents of modern educational practices. Accepting small-group instruction and learning as valid, however, has meant that students and teachers alike have found it necessary to abandon the security of many traditional concepts. Exploring the unknown has been difficult, sometimes frightening, and often frustrating. Progress has been slow or unnoticeable. Yet today at Marshall, although small-group instruction has not reached the heavenly state of perfection described by its prominent advocates, there exists little doubt that small groups do provide students with a unique opportunity for intellectual and behavioral development.

IN THE BEGINNING

Anticipation of meeting students in groups of fifteen or less led some teachers to envision a sort of educational utopia where, at last, great amounts of knowledge could be imparted to the student. Teachers who interpreted small-group instruction in this manner found the vision fading as they discovered both the impracticability and impossibility of covering the same body of knowledge in small groups meeting two or three times a week for forty minutes each, as had been taught one hour a day, five days a week.

The admonitions of J. Lloyd Trump that small groups should be a setting for free and open exchange of ideas among students, should provide for problem solving and exploration, and should provide opportunity for students to direct their own learning seemed to be in direct contrast to many of the practices going on in small groups. The traditional dominant role assumed by teachers, in which questions originated from the teacher and responses were returned to the teacher, seemed to discourage discussion.

Some teachers, uneasy that they were not fulfilling the promises of small groups, questioned their own approaches and methods and began an exploration of possibilities which could turn theory into sound practice. Questions arose to which there seemed no ready answers.

1. How do students learn discussion techniques most effectively?
2. How much does the teacher talk in the small group and when?
3. Should discussion topics in small groups be directly related to and an outgrowth of large-group presentations?
4. How much free choice should students have in determining their topics of discussion?

These and other questions indicated that both students and teachers needed assistance in determining how they might utilize small groups most effectively. As a result, a small-group action-research committee was formed. Experiments were designed to discover what kinds of learning could occur in small groups and how groups could be evaluated for these learnings. Members of the committee visited one another's groups frequently, consulting afterward to exchange observations, questions, fears, and possible ideas. By the end of the first year, the committee had reached at least one important milestone—an awareness of group processes and human interaction.

At the same time, a small-group research committee served as a clearinghouse for research findings on such topics as group processes, group sizes, and role of the leader in groups, and also for techniques which had been tried by teachers in their own small groups. Dissemination of this information to members of the faculty served to stimulate experiment with, and interest in, small groups.

Although concern about small-group learning was general throughout the faculty, not all departments within the school utilized small-group time for discussion and exploration. In the music department, for example, small-group meetings provided opportunity for section rehearsals for band and chorus. In the foreign language department, on the other hand, small groups seemed best suited for individual audio-lingual practice in the language. For some departments, such as art, which utilized laboratory to a great extent, small groups were not formally scheduled. Mathematics small groups provided students with an opportunity to obtain additional teacher help. For these departments, the small-group problems which confronted the areas of English, social studies, or science did not exist.

In spite of attempts of the committees and others to offer some suggested guidelines for small-group operation, teacher reaction to the new demands made and new skills required for that phase of instruction varied. Reactions ranged from (1) rejection of the whole notion of student-centered discussions as balderdash and misspent time when the trained teacher knowledgeable in his own field was obviously the one who could dispense this information more efficently, to (2) cautious experimentation with semidirected activities in which students assumed responsibility at the teacher's discretion and with teacher-developed ideas, to (3) "whole-hog" acceptance of the concept of free student-centered discussions.

Acceptance of the idea of small-group learning meant a vis-à-vis encounter with several disturbing discoveries. First of all, the teacher was cast in a variety of new roles. No longer in a dominant position in the small group, the teacher became listener, participant, consultant, observer, discussion leader, or general healer. (See Figure 3-1.) For teachers accustomed to doing more than 50 percent of the talking in classes, such an adjustment was not easily made.

Similarly students, unaccustomed to the image of their teachers in this less directive role, persistently sought signs of approval

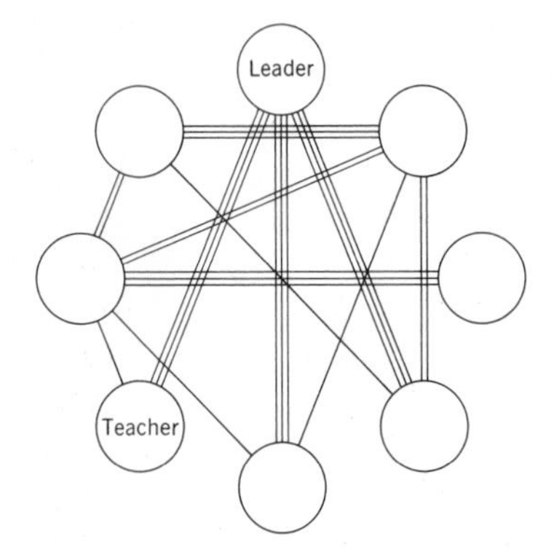

Teacher as participant

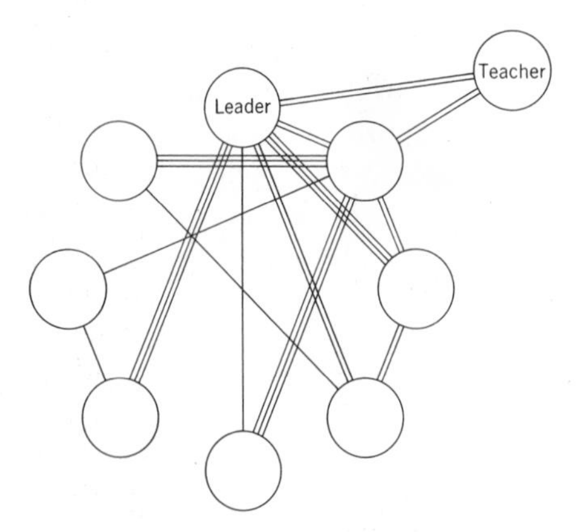

Teacher as observer and consultant

FIGURE 3-1. Two different roles of the teacher in small groups

or disapproval. It was unlikely that a free flow of ideas would develop in a discussion group punctuated by smiles, nods, or frowns from the teacher. In essence, the teacher who behaved in that way had never relinquished direct control of the group. Establishing an atmosphere of freedom and trust among students when they were accustomed to right and wrong answers was a delicate, difficult task.

In order to establish this feeling in small groups, a prerequisite to successful accomplishment of any work, varieties of techniques were tried. "Icebreakers," or nonthreatening topics, to which there obviously were no "acceptable" or "unacceptable" answers seemed to be successful. In several social studies small groups, for example, students were given a hypothetical case study posing a moral dilemma which forced students to decide which of several persons would be allowed in a fallout shelter during a nuclear attack.

Interest in the case study permitted the teacher to act as observer, listening for statements which reflected student attitudes and feelings about themselves and others and noting the manner in which they related to each other, their ability to verbalize, and possible leadership potential.

Once the climate of free expression was established, it was possible to concentrate on the two remaining areas of small-group concern, subject matter and group processes. Which should receive priority? Both students and teachers were subject-matter oriented. Students felt that if they were not doing "a lot of reading and writing," they were not learning. Talking was all right, but when did the real schoolwork begin? The reaction of one ninth-grade boy to small-group discussion reflects the prevailing feeling among students at the outset of the year. "Small groups are when uninformed students and an opinionated teacher sit around talking about important things they don't know anything about or trivial things that don't matter."

Indoctrinated to the notion that all direction must come from the teacher and that all ideas must fit into a category of right and wrong, students were unable and unwilling to accept the responsibility of making choices. As a result, teachers found it necessary to devote much small-group meeting time to the examination of the goals and objectives of the course, to actual evaluation of the discussions, and to the task of learning to discuss effectively by "doing." Students, like teachers, were inexperienced in this type of learning situation and certainly inexperienced in accepting the responsibility for their own learning.

Faced with these new challenges, teachers drew upon their creative resources, attempting to find approaches and techniques which would make small groups "go." Although individual successes appeared in isolated small groups, they were, generally, unsatisfactory learning situations. The chief barriers to effective small-group instruction seemed to be:

1. Students had difficulty in accepting the role of discussion leader or recorder. These roles precluded active participation in discussion, and students wanted to talk. Perhaps it was a lack of maturity; perhaps it was discovery of a newfound freedom of expression which none of them wished to relinquish.
2. Students often made elaborate plans for study, but frequently had difficulty in following through. Teachers were faced with the question, "Should I tell the group these plans may not be workable, or should I let them find out for themselves?"
3. Students had difficulty in developing a feeling of responsibility for group outcomes. Confronted at the outset of their planning sessions with the job of goal setting, most small groups regarded this as a formality designed to please the teacher. This seemed to be particularly true in groups which operated within a semistructured situation, in which students had limited choices of discussion and study topics or problems to solve. Students in less structured groups, who were given greater latitude of choice, often became more involved in their group problem and assumed greater responsibility for the success or failure of the study.
4. Students often came to the small group unprepared for discussion, having given it neither prior thought nor study.

Several factors seemed to have been responsible for this. First, students had not learned to use their independent-study time to best advantage. Assignments made by the group were often last-minute afterthoughts and were seldom clarified. Students had not accepted the importance of small-group discussion.

5. Teachers were uncertain as to whether time limits for a given topic of study should be a student or a teacher decision. Time limits were often a barrier to creativity and real interest in some groups. Conversely, time limits forced some groups to pursue a topic beyond their point of saturation.

6. Group conflicts often impeded intellectual progress of the group. Teachers, unskilled for the most part in group dynamics and group interaction, were uncertain as to how much they should involve the group in identifying and working with the problem of personality conflict. Teachers were confronted with such questions as, "Should this group subdivide if it cannot function effectively as a whole? Should I change the members of this group as a possible solution? Should I put the decision before the group for consideration?"

7. Student choices of study with only broad limitations to guide them implied a wide variety of curricular choices. Some teachers had as many as ten small groups working in different areas of a problem or reading different selections at the same time. Teachers questioned if this freedom might not result in a chaotic curriculum.

8. Given choices, students often requested controversial books or chose to discuss controversial issues. Although discussion of controverial issues was generally encouraged by teachers, assigning of controversial books—sometimes in general disfavor within the district—presented a minor dilemma for teachers and administrators.

9. Some students were shaken by the new image of their teachers in a less directive role. Some lacked confidence in their

ability to function under a less structured situation. Some became surly and hostile toward the teacher for placing them in this position of responsibility. A ninth-grade boy, for example, shaken from his comfortable security when informed by the teacher that the members of the small group would be responsible for determining their own report-card grades, confronted the teacher with, "How dare you place this responsibility on us! It's your job to grade us. That's what you're paid for. You have no right to do this to us."

10. Less able students, who were usually unable to meet with any kind of academic success in school, did not function in the same manner as more capable ones, particularly if they were expected to supply their own structure. Group interaction was often of a physical nature, and students experienced more difficulty in seeing possibilities for discussion.

As these and other problems became increasingly apparent, teachers continued their experimentation and investigation—themselves learning to view failures as a step toward possible success. Because of the quixotic nature of small-group behavior, conclusions and observations which grew out of small-group experiments were of a tentative sort, subject to constant reappraisal.

HOW FAR HAVE WE COME?

From the beginning, it has been obvious that students must be aware of and understand the significance of the part each member of the small group plays in achieving effectiveness. The reponsibilities of the leader, the recorder, the observer, and the participant must be understood by all members. Although primary emphasis has been placed upon development of individuals as participants, attention has also been given to development of leadership in groups.

In order to facilitate this, leadership in the group is sometimes rotated, so that each person may experience the problems and responsibilities of the leader. Sometimes groups function with permanent student leaders. Serving the group as recorder or observer is often on a rotation basis also. In all cases, students carrying out these duties in their groups meet with the teachers in conference to discuss necessary procedures and methods of performing their task effectively. These approaches are especially favored by teachers of incoming ninth-grade students, unfamiliar with the ways of small groups.

Most valuable of all methods has been constant student-teacher appraisal and evaluation during the discussions. If this occurs frequently in the early stages of group development, less time seems to be required for this process as members become more sophisticated in group processes. Devices most frequently utilized as kickoff points for evaluation are flow charts, tape recordings of discussions, verbatim minutes of small-group meetings, and feedback from an observer.

Flow charts, which may be recorded by student or teacher, provide a record of (1) the number of contributions made by each individual and whether the contribution is relevant to the topic and made to the group, to his neighbor, or is unrelated to the subject under discussion; or (2) the direction of the flow of discussion. (See Figure 3-2.) From the chart, it is possible to offer a visual picture of group procedure. Tape recordings of discussions, which provide an opportunity for analysis, may be placed in the resource center, where students often choose to listen to the discussion again during independent-study time. Verbatim minutes of a small-group meeting, although difficult to accomplish unless the recorder is a speedwriter, is an effective tool for evaluating when read back to the group or duplicated for members to examine. Perhaps the best record of small-group performance is a video-tape recording. The playback of such a record is enlightening to both teacher and students.

Whatever the instrument for evaluation, the benefit to the group comes from a penetrating examination of group progress or lack of it. From such sessions often result group recommendations about procedures which should and should not be followed. For example, one small group at Marshall decided that the most effective way to achieve its goal of understanding the important aspects of the culture of India was to study and discuss every phase of Indian life. At the end of four weeks, after

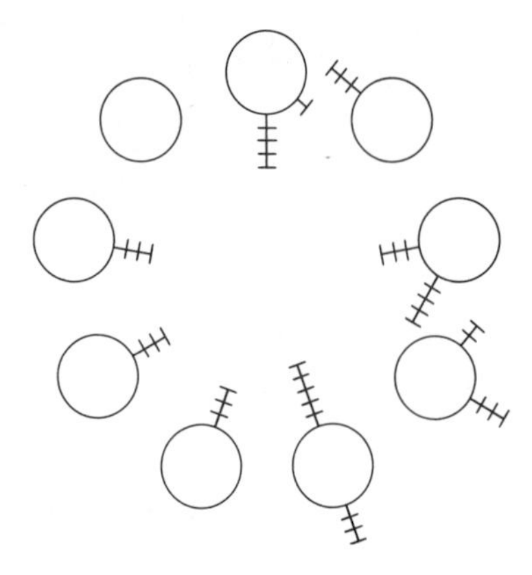

Flow chart designed to show number of relevant contributions made to group, number of irrelevant contributions made to group, and side exchanges

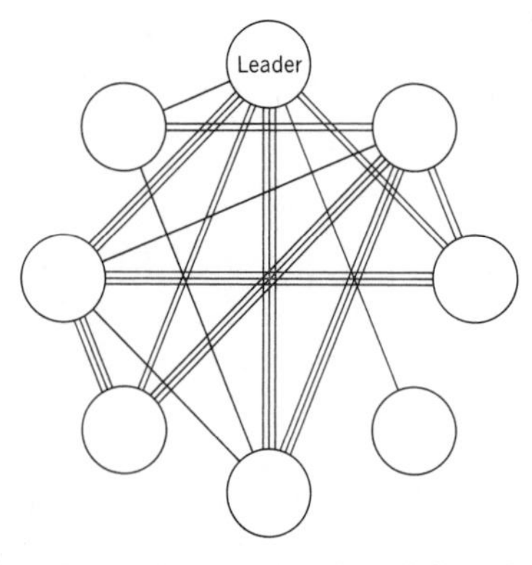

Flow chart designed to show flow of discussion

FIGURE 3-2. Discussion flow charts in small groups

plowing laboriously through geography, history, customs, politics, etc., the group called a halt to proceedings in order to evaluate its progress. The follow-up discussions indicated that members felt they had tried to cover too much subject matter and that they had not really thought very deeply about nor investigated other possibilities of real interest to them. Furthermore, they concluded that if they took a closer look at Hinduism as a way of life they might accomplish the same goal and find greater stimulation at the same time. During the preliminary planning sessions of this group, the teacher had been undecided about whether the group should be informed of the possibility of failure with their approach or whether they should continue until they discovered for themselves that they had undertaken a cumbersome task not entirely to their liking.

Interestingly enough, however, teachers are not always expert judges as to whether a decision made by a group will end in failure. A ninth-grade English small group composed of slow learners complained about the "childish" literature given to them to read. What they really wanted to read, they said, was *Huck Finn,* a selection read by the ninth-grade college-capable students. Despite discouraging words from the teacher about the difficulty of the dialect and the problems of length of the selection, the group persisted in its request.

Consequently, a copy of *The Adventures of Huckleberry Finn* was given to each member of the group, and plans were made for discussion leaders and for discussion questions. (Incidentally, the teacher had voiced to her colleagues the certainty that this venture would end in a smashing failure within two weeks.)

The group did not fail. Not only did members of the group make reading assignments for each session, but the leader came prepared each time with discussion questions based on the reading. Entire small-group sessions were spent puzzling over and interpreting the dialect. The enthusiasm, the determination of students, and the level of the discussions were more than the teacher had thought possible. Perhaps the motivation came from a desire for equal intellectual status with better students, or perhaps the group wanted to prove to the teacher that they could meet the challenge and succeed, or perhaps they really wanted to read the book.

Permitting students to make decisions and then follow through to experience the natural consequences of the decisions has given students a feeling of real involvement and has been, in part, responsible for the development of a higher degree of accountability for the outcomes of the group. Shielding students from failure or from the consequences of a poor decision denies them the most valuable aspect of the experience. Without this phase, true understanding of what they have been doing does not come. Small groups then become a place to talk about problems and solutions, rather than a place to experience them. Evaluations written at the end of the year by students have revealed repeatedly that the sense of responsibility for group success or failure increases in proportion to the degree of involvement. Although students may be critical of teacher efforts in large groups, they are equally critical of their own efforts in small groups.

Lest it appear that students can operate at optimum effectiveness without guidance or assistance from the teacher, it should be mentioned that students in groups in which the teacher has played a passive, nonparticipating role have often lost their sense of purpose, have meandered, and have become confused and often uninterested. A constant examination by students and teachers of the purposes of the study seems essential, for students themselves say that they need this constant reminder of the direction in which they are moving. Groups often request teacher assistance in determining suitable topics for discussion, clarification of terms or policy, or unearthing of sources of information, if it is not forthcoming when it is needed.

Another problem faced by students and teachers in small-group learning situations, and one more difficult to resolve, has been that of personality and group conflict. Because teachers have felt inadequately trained in dealing with problems of this nature and because students often find it difficult, if not impossible, to express personal feelings about members of the group, these areas of discontent are often left unresolved with a resulting detriment to group progress.

Those at Marshall who have reported some success in dealing with this aspect of group interaction are quick to admit that the conflicts can only be discussed if there is a high degree of trust among members of the group (teacher included). Students must know that whatever they say will not cause them to be outcasts in the group. They must know that they will not be ridiculed, and they must certainly feel that there is some real value in talking about the feelings which are standing in the way of effective group participation.

Perhaps the following excerpts from the minutes of two meetings of a small group will make clear the effect personal conflict can have upon group progress. This particular small group was composed of twelve mature, confident ninth graders who respected and accepted one another. When confronted with the problem, they were able to examine it and talk about it, although unable to arrive at a solution.

JAN. 22 MEETING:

> Since members will be evaluating themselves, they felt a final test was not necessary. Teacher asked how they would be able to judge their understandings and learnings without a final test. Members felt that a final discussion would reveal these. Karen objected to this indicating that she found it very difficult to talk in this group, although she had no difficulty in her other small groups. She said she felt she was not as "smart" as other members. Cathy said she, too, felt uncomfortable about saying anything in front of Mona and Holly because they were "brains." Holly indicated that she often felt inferior to others, and that Cathy had no need to feel inadequate. . . .

(*Note:* Mona said nothing to these charges.)

FEB. 5 MEETING:

> Teacher informed the group that Karen wished to leave the group because she felt so uncomfortable. Karen related her feelings to the group. She said she felt inadequate and uncomfortable because she was unable to contribute anything to the discussion. She felt that anything she had to say was already known by all other members. Karen said that her feelings were related primarily to one person in the group, but she was unwilling to reveal the name of that person.
>
> Group reaction was mixed. Most members wanted to know who the individual was. Some felt the problem was Karen's to solve and were not sure how the group could help. Peggy said she thought the group should be concerned since the problem

> affected all of them. Rick was concerned that Karen was embarrassed by the "ordeal."
>
> Cathy said she felt much as Karen did, and often didn't understand what was being said in the group. Holly related that she felt that way too when she wasn't involved in the discussion, but that participating often helped her to understand by speaking her thoughts.
>
> Tim pointed out to Karen that everyone has strengths and weaknesses and she should search herself for her strengths and not dwell so much on what she felt were inadequacies.
>
> Generally, the group felt that Karen needed to reassure herself and indicated that if she left, some members would feel it was their fault. Gordon said that if she left, he would *know* that he was the reason she was going. . . .

(*Note:* The person who had such an impact on Karen was Mona, who had remained silent during both discussions, although she was usually talkative. She was aware that she was the center of the problem. In subsequent conferences, the teacher and the two girls were able to talk out the problem to the satisfaction of both.)

Another excerpt from the minutes of that group indicates how the behavior and desires of one individual were successful in blocking group progress.

MARCH 5 MEETING:

> Gordon objected to the term *civilization* and suggested that *society* be used. According to him, *Lord of the Flies* did not reflect civilization. He asked for a definition of the two terms. The group felt it was not necessary. . . .
>
> Gordon interjected that personality of people in novels had a bearing on the development of society. Group rejected this statement as not apropos. . . .
>
> Gordon suggested again that this small group could be a criterion for deciding what constitutes a society. Group rejected idea.
>
> Gordon disagreed. He felt that class was determined by prestige.

> Gordon called for defining of society again. He insisted that it was not off the subject under discussion.
>
> Several side discussions broke out at this point. Group ignored Gordon's request and continued discussion.
>
> Gordon and Floyd became involved at this point in a side discussion of *society* versus *civilization*. Discussion finally involved all members of the group.

In spite of group rejection, Gordon won that round! Gordon's ideas were generally rejected by the group as being inappropriate. The group (and Gordon) seemed aware that his role in that group was "blocker." The group accepted Gordon on these terms, and Gordon seldom seemed deterred by their frequent rejection of his ideas.

However, not all groups have the maturity and confidence needed to recognize and discuss such problems. In another small group, less mature and more conforming, every effort to come to group consensus on any topic ended in a sarcastic interchange between members. Individually, members of the group admitted feelings of hostility toward others in the group, but they could never bring themselves to talk about it in group meetings. Because no other solution could be found to help this group operate more efficiently, the group subdivided.

Subdivision often occurred when consensus could not be reached on a given topic or area of study and a substantial number of group members wished to pursue some other area. Groups usually chose to settle these questions by majority rule in the beginning but soon discovered that if group consensus was not reached, the entire venture could be undermined by those who did not want to do it in the first place.

Conflict problems in groups also may be resolved by retaining a high degree of flexibility in group membership. By moving one member of a small group to another group, both individual and group may operate more effectively. An example of this occurred in an English small group dominated by a confident, knowledgeable, and very verbal girl. The thirteen other members seldom talked. After watching the group disintegrate slowly to the point of monologue by the talkative member, the teacher finally confronted her with a choice of remaining in that group or transferring to a group composed of other talkative students. She was willing and delighted to move to the other group. When the remaining members of the group were asked for their reaction to this move, they breathed a collective sigh of relief. "Now we can talk without feeling like idiots." After Sue's transfer, the remainder of the group participated actively in discussion. They had not been able to express their apprehensions and concerns, but their actions and reactions were telling enough for the most insensitive teacher to observe.

As would be imagined, each small group reflects its own individual personality and must certainly be granted individual dignity. No one solution to group problems, whether intellectual or emotional, can be prescribed for all groups. In one small group, the girls expressed a dislike for working with the boys, who were interested in more intellectual topics generally than the girls. No amount of talking could resolve this problem, so the girls became a subgroup and the boys remained together. However, within their group of nine, only five boys seemed to be active in discussion. The other four were always silent. After some soul-searching, the teacher further subdivided the boys, giving the four quiet boys their own group status. To the amazement of all, the one boy who had said nothing all year in group discussions emerged as the leader of the four and became the most talkative member of the subgroup.

Such subdivisions solve problems, but create new ones for the teacher. It is difficult to observe closely more than one group at a time. Subdivision means that a group will be alone at least half the time. If one of the subdivisions has more difficulties and problems than the others, it is possible that the teacher might spend a disproportionate amount of time with that one, thus neglecting the others.

Recognizing the individuality of each small group has created the problem of diversity of content materials. Some teachers have avoided this problem by insisting that all students use the same materials. Others limit choices to a few topics or books. But in the small groups in which students are given a wide latitude, students often choose materials with which the teacher is unfamiliar or which are controversial. Some teachers feel it is a sign of ineffectiveness if the teacher is not familiar with all materials utilized by students. Others, whose students frequently are working with materials and books new to them, report they find an excitement in investigating along with the student.

As one would expect, students at Marshall High School have shown interest in controversial issues and readings, as do most high school students. Because there exists within the district and within the school a fairly high degree of academic freedom, students are encouraged to examine the controversial. On occasion, students select books which are in general disfavor within the school district. They sometimes circumvent problems of district objections by buying their own copies, reading the books outside of class, and using small-group discussion time for examination of the ideas within the book pertinent to their study.

The question of the need for structure in small-group learning has been and continues to be the most controversial aspect of this phase of the program. Although there is general agreement that bright, capable students are able to benefit from a situation which permits them to exercise self-direction and planning, teachers are sharply divided in their small-group philosophies for average and below-average students. Less confident, less able, and younger students frequently have been overcome by the responsibility of facing so many decisions. Rather than developing independence, they have often become fearful of their inadequacy to stand on their own and accept responsibility for their own learning.

For the most part, teachers seem to feel that a close relationship between large group and small group should exist and that students benefit from definite assignments which show the tie between the two. Students seem to sense the continuity more strongly when they understand the relationship of the several phases of a course. From experiences of teachers at all grade levels and in most subject fields, it appears that students who are not highly motivated or self-directed function most effectively when confronted with only a few decisions and choices in the beginning. Some students continue to require the reassurance of more structure and direction from the teachers throughout the year. Slow learners, for the most part, have been unable to perform in an effective manner outside a structured classroom situation. Even in the individualized atmosphere of small groups, using the same methods for all students is no more effective than it was in the traditional classroom.

Although no statistical compilations which prove the value of small-group instruction exist at Marshall, observations and subjective evaluations made by students and teachers, and sometimes by parents, would indicate that some gains have been made in developing independence and self-direction in learning. The feelings of a concerned but enlightened parent of a freshman at the beginning of last year were revealed thus: "It pleases me that the students have opportunities for development of self-reliance in learning through discovery themselves, but is there a body of knowledge which my son will need in order to provide background for other social studies courses or for college?" Later in the year the same parent made the following comment: "I can see now that learning how to learn independently is what students should be striving for and that the subject matter used is unimportant."

The following observable changes in student behavior and attitudes toward learning seem widespread enough to justify the validity of small-group instruction:

1. Students have developed a sense of responsibility for their own learning. They are more able to make plans and evaluate outcomes. They make mistakes, as do their teachers, but in the process have become more analytical and honestly critical about their own efforts. They have shown an ability to make decisions, sometimes in spite of teachers, and follow through successfully on these decisions.
2. Students have learned to think independently of the teachers. More and more, they have come to accept the teacher in her varied roles and less and less seek to parrot what teachers expect. Teachers, too, have become more skilled in handling their diverse roles and have developed a fairly high degree of acceptance for divergent ideas. Speculation on the part of students is less often regarded as "silly non-

sense" than it once was, as teachers have developed greater skill in leading such speculation to some educated conclusions.

3. Students have become more confident in the validity of their own ideas, and in themselves as individuals.
4. Students learn from each other as they question in small groups. Questions once directed to the teacher are now directed to other members of the group.
5. Students have become more skilled in dialogue with each other and have developed greater awareness of the possibilities for learning. Exposure to other small groups through frequent visitation and exposure to diverse ideas within their own small groups have opened new vistas and broadened the outlook of many students.
6. Teachers have become more acutely aware of individual and group problems as they have come to accept themselves as listeners.
7. Discipline problems, found frequently in traditionally sized classes, are nonexistent in small groups. Size is one factor, but more important is the group pressure exerted on the deviant.
8. Teachers have generally become more flexible in their regard for subject matter.
9. Students and teachers alike have become more aware of the goals and objectives toward which they are working.
10. Students, because of an increased involvement in their own learning, have shown greater interest in their schoolwork.

WHERE DO WE GO FROM HERE?

Change brings with it many rewards, but it does not guarantee the elimination of all problems. Although small-group instruction has undoubtedly solved some old problems, it has emphasized others and perhaps has created new ones. Still perplexing members of the faculty are such problems as the following:

1. Drawing quiet and reticent students into discussion is still

a problem. More important, teachers ask if all students should be expected to discuss effectively. Is this, in fact, denying their individuality if they are not able to participate?

2. A long period of indoctrination will be required before all students feel the importance of dialogue as a means of learning.
3. In an effort to motivate small groups into involvement, curriculum has in some instances been developed within each small group, sometimes resulting in such fragmentation that students feel as though the three phases of a course are actually three different courses. Maintaining curricular organization seems important for continuity; yet can this be accomplished without limiting the creativity of students and teachers?
4. Still the most pressing problem facing the entire staff is the question of motivation of students. It is, in reality, a summary of all the other problems which remain unsolved. For the bright, for the motivated student, small groups offer endless possibilities. But what of the average, bored, unmotivated student? Can he, too, become so involved in some aspect of school and learning that he begins to care?

The following memorandum from one Marshall teacher to the principal suggests that such motivation is possible, if one is willing to pay the price demanded. Submitted as a progress report by Mrs. Patricia Baars, a ninth-grade social studies teacher, the letter refers to an experiment involving a small group of bored, average-ability students, some of whom were frequently absent from class and whose report-card grades up to that time were all C's, D's, and F's. The project grew out of a group reaction to Mrs. Baars' questions, "Why are you here if social studies offers nothing you need or want? What would you do if you were in a position in which you could really control your grades, your attendance, and all your learning?"

After admitting her inability to teach by force, Mrs. Baars indicated that the members of that group no longer need come if they felt it was of no value. Several indicated that they might not. However, subsequent meetings found them back in small group. Mrs. Baars offered them another challenge. "Assuming you have returned because you feel the class might become useful or interesting now, what do you want to do to bring this about?" Several meetings later, the students decided her offer was "for real" and began what ultimately became an exciting study of the city of Portland—its history, architecture, renovation, and functions—complete with over one hundred self-made slides, showing change in various areas over time. Students located and selected old pictures from various community sources, made them into slides, and then made a corresponding set of new slides showing the same areas at the present time.

At the end of the year, after four and a half months of work, several members of the small group were so involved in the study that they asked to be helped to continue their work in the summer and through the next school year as a voluntary group-study project. In their words, they had "only scratched the surface" of their topic. Mrs. Baars' memorandum to the principal follows:

> Your interest in the City of Portland Project of my Small Group 6 has prompted me to send in a progress report because I'm itching to tell somebody what I think I've learned about motivating average-ability, bored students. I'm as startled as anybody that they want to continue their project next year, and I have been talking informally to some of them in conference about just what it is that "set them off" in this particular class situation. These conversations, plus my observations and midnight thoughts, have led me to these tentative conclusions: First, that student refusal to become interested is very often a defense against disappointment. These students are all too familiar with parents and teachers who make big plans and then fail to follow through on promises—or who dampen student-originated enthusiasm with neat, logical reasons why prior plans can't be changed. Whatever else it is, a project as ambitious as the Portland study is bound to be a big bother to parents and teachers asked to furnish transportation, permission for this and that, money for films, and so forth. And if we feel that we don't

want to be bothered, this message comes through loud and clear to the student. Second, students feel that learning ("real" learning, that is) has to be painful. I've heard teachers say, "You need to learn that education is hard, hard work!" So have they. And they believe, by the time they're fourteen, that it is *nothing but* hard work—work that, furthermore, doesn't pay off. Third, students will not work for, nor enjoy learning from, someone who does not feel respect for them. And I mean respect, not maudlin affection. I wouldn't know how to encourage anybody to respect another person. Some teachers respect their students, some do not, and most don't change from one attitude to the other. I don't know how I came to respect these particular students; perhaps it was because I took enough time really to know them and to listen to them, and to convince them I had something to learn from them; and sooner or later I realized that we were much more alike than we were different, which is reassuring to all concerned, I think. Respecting a student involves being willing to trust him with making many of his own decisions; perhaps in this project "acting" as if I respected them, in the beginning, made them "respectable." Fourth, students like this are almost certain to be suspicious of the teacher's motives ("What's in it for her?"). I would advise anyone who tries a project like this to be very honest with himself, as well as with students, about motives. Students who are somewhat rebellious about school aren't going to be very cooperative about "falling for another gimmick" just to gratify teacher's ego. The student who said, "I know your angle—you're just using reverse psychology on us!" was looking for my gimmick. The teacher had best respond with honest discussion, not touchiness, when areas like this are probed. Fifth, rewards for the students need to be as immediate as possible, especially for freshmen. If you say to them, "Think big—how do you know what might not be possible?" be prepared to take action soon. Class discussions full of "Wouldn't it be great if we could . . ." need to be followed up immediately by concrete sounding out of people, possibilities, and so forth. The teacher must act, at first, as the student's door-opener to the outside world. At first, the planning should come from students, and the teacher is the errand-runner—not the other way around. This is contrary to some teachers' notions, I know. All I can say in defense of it is that it works, and soon students are doing both jobs. Here is an example: about three weeks ago, in a Wednesday small group meeting, they were discussing how best to complete the tedious chore of sorting, classifying and map-locating about 100 pictures. Thirty-six hours later, most of the class was at my house for the afternoon doing the job, having returned signed permission slips, divided and completed the job of buying and bringing all the food for a spaghetti dinner, and arranged for transportation home. In four hours *they* finished the picture chore, cooked and ate dinner and went home, having had a little fun on the side. The reward, of course, was in taking an active part in carrying out an ambitious plan, made by themselves, on short notice—and in the telling of the tale to envious friends the next day. The sixth motivating factor is making the students, as an experimental group, somewhat unique, and therefore, conspicuous. This raises a question—if uniqueness is an important motivating factor, could all students be involved? Only, I think, if each group is treated as completely separate from all the others and allowed to develop in its own way according to the needs of its own members. But one problem makes this project approach impossible for a teacher to use with all classes; and this is the demand which commitment to this kind of thing makes upon the teacher in terms of time and effort. It simply could not be done with student loads as heavy as they are now, if the quality of effort is to be that which produces substantial results. I'm not at all sure I'm happy to know how very well this approach works; now I have to decide who gets the chance and who doesn't.

The tentative conclusions of one teacher about motivational factors involved with the success of a small group may have implications far beyond Small Group 6—implications for instructional methods and curriculum, for development of true sensitivity and awareness of student needs and concerns, for development of attitudes among students. If these observations and conclusions have any validity, like Small Group 6, the teachers at Marshall have only begun to "scratch the surface" of small-group possibilities.

4

Independent Study: Projects

Gary Cummings

The atmosphere established at Marshall is clearly intended to provide the greatest possibility for independent thinking and individual development in both students and teachers. And certainly this is just the kind of atmosphere one should expect in a school. Few would disagree that the end of all education should be a curious, imaginative, and intelligent human being. All the reverence afforded the term *individual differences* must be evidence of the universality of that goal. Unfortunately, some shadowy negative connotation has adhered to the term. Many seem to feel that individual differences are those unforeseen disasters which thwart *real education.* Here, of course, real education means the mastery of mathematics, English, or history. In this conception of education, the means and ends of education are somehow confused, and individual differences as they relate to total human development are largely ignored. At Marshall we are not abandoning or disparaging the academic disciplines. Their lasting importance is recognized by all, but we are trying to correct the confusion of means and ends of education that is so apparent in much of the academic world. We are trying to use what is new in our school to alter the academic system, to make it more productive of curiosity, imagination, and intelligence than it has been in the past.

Instead of viewing individual differences as something to be overcome on the way to education, we are trying to find ways of making the development of individuality the most important part of the educational experience. To this end we have instituted as an integral part of our established curriculum another dimension called *independent study.* Although this term is certainly not new and has recently gained in popularity, its meaning at Marshall is, as far as we know, unique. Independent study is our attempt to deal as adequately as possible with real individual differences and to provide exciting learning experiences for every student, regardless of his ability or his interests.

In the independent-study project, one of the major elements of the whole independent-study program, the *student* decides what he is interested in and uses that interest to gain knowledge and to exercise his creative and organizational powers. The independent-study project, if it is given enough weight and respect in the school, should often tap latent abilities and allow achievement which leads to greater commitment to the school as a whole.

THE COMPLICATIONS

Obviously, the implementation of this new dimension has necessitated some important changes in teacher and student attitudes toward the curriculum and toward education in general. If independent study is going to be truly important, if it is even to begin to accomplish what we hope it can, in some cases teachers must be prepared to see their subject fields from new perspectives. That is, even though a teacher may have prepared himself to teach a given concept in a certain way and the school system suggests a certain procedure for teaching the concept, if a student becomes really involved in an independent-study project that is clearly leading to the goals stated above, the teacher should be prepared to find a way to make that student's enthusiasm for his project result in improved learning of the desired academic concepts. Almost all subjects are conceptually related. If a teacher is prepared to help a student find those relationships in an imaginative manner, the independent-study project can be a richly rewarding learning experience. Not only must a teacher relinquish his old ideas about subject-matter isolation, but he must also discard many of his old methods of motivating, directing, or evaluating his students. It is possible in independent study that a teacher's best student may not even be enrolled in his classes. A student may choose a teacher as his independent-study-project adviser because of a former acquaintance or because the teacher has special ability, knowledge, or interests relevant to the student's project. The teacher-student relationship under these conditions is much different from the conventional classroom relationship, and possibly much more rewarding.

Students also find themselves confronted with problems much different from those they would encounter in a conventional program. Because teachers hope to use independent study to stimulate original and creative thought, students must learn not to expect many specific instructions or directions. The teacher's role here is not to tell the student what to do or really how to do it. The teacher acts much as a resource person, helping the student to clarify his ideas and to analyze his problems as he meets them and trying to show the student how and where to find materials relevant to his project. The role is more like that of the midwife who aids in delivery than that of the farmer who plants and harvests.

Since grades play no significant role in the independent-study project, students are forced to find within themselves the motivation for success in whatever they choose to do. They often discover that they need the help of teachers from two or more disciplines in accomplishing their goals, and consequently they must consider their projects from several points of view and discuss their problems with several personalities. The organizational problems the student encounters in a project are admittedly more complex than those he would meet in a conventional curriculum, and some students do find them insuperable the first time they try a project. We are sure, however, that for those who honestly attempt the independent project, the learning experience is often much richer than that in a conventional program and that for those who find success, the feeling of achievement is deeper and more rewarding. The successful students in independent study, and these are not necessarily the best students academically, gain pride in accomplishment as well as the knowledge that their ideas and interests are important.

FIRST STEPS

When we first began to investigate independent study at Marshall, we realized that good communication among the faculty, between the faculty and the students, and in the larger context of the total school community was essential to success. If students were to have the freedom of inquiry we envisioned, they would need the cooperation of many teachers. Again, if students were to understand fully the implications of their new opportunities, all their teachers would have to be aware of some basic ideas about independent study. We were aware that independent study would force more students to seek individual conferences and that teachers would have to be prepared for this increased demand on their time. Teachers would also have to find time to discuss student projects with co-advisers. But most importantly, we had to find a means of making independent study a schoolwide interest. Obviously, conventional communication channels would have to be improved and new channels opened.

At this point, few of us had given much effort to formulating any organized method of approaching independent study. In the first year of our new program, a small group of teachers had worked with Dr. Richard Boyd, district director for staff development, experimenting in independent study with a limited number of students, but there had been little effort to make independent study an integral part of our total curriculum. Then James Barchek, English department chairman, and a group of English teachers who felt a need for exploring the possibilities of independent study initiated the Independent Study Committee. The committee met in the evenings in teachers' homes to develop an approach to independent study and to outline a program for its success.

Our first concern was to develop an adequate and common understanding of what we were attempting. Few of us were in complete agreement on the meaning of independent study, and our attempts to compile a bibliography and to get help from other schools were practically fruitless. The schools with which we corresponded had either not developed an independent-study program, or if they had, their ideas were not relevant to the unique conditions we faced. Most of the written material pertinent to our ideas of independent study had come, we found, from the "Marshall Press," a mimeograph machine in our main office. One of the more significant documents was a definition of independent study developed by Dr. Boyd's earlier committee. We all found it compatible with our ideas, and it gave us a concrete basis for future development. It read as follows:

Definition of Independent Study

Independent study is a method of self-development and personal growth. It involves choosing a problem or topic which has particular meaning for the individual and following it to a point where it satisfies his curiosity or need at the time.

The student:

(1) Chooses the problem or topic

(2) Decides how he will investigate,

  (*a*) Alone or with others

  (*b*) Reading, interview, observation, experimentation

(3) Reports progress

  (*a*) To the teacher

  (*b*) To others who are interested

The group of teachers who helped formulate this definition was primarily interested in the project aspect of independent study, and they were trying to arrive at a basis for discussion of the problems they were encountering in experimental classes. Thus the definition is fairly abstract and more prescriptive than descriptive. It does, however, imply some basic assumptions about learning and about the attitudes and goals of students which we all agreed were essential to the larger subject of independent study at Marshall. After many of us had actually worked with our students in independent study and after the school had become somewhat adjusted to the idea of independent time for students, we wrote a more specific and descriptive definition of independent study as it exists at Marshall; and the above definition then became only that of the independent-study *project.* One of the major differences between the earlier definition and this description is that the latter includes many aspects of a student's endeavors that have nothing to do with a project. The comprehensive definition as presented to, and adopted by, the faculty reads as follows:

Independent Study

The title of this paper is a very broad term which means many different things to many people. The following is an attempt to explore the significance of this term for Marshall High School.

Independent Study itself refers to a student's constructive use of unscheduled time. The Independent Study Committee has attempted to survey Marshall's program to discover what opportunities are available for our students. Below is a partial classification and description of these opportunities.

A. Homework (any work assigned as a regular part of the curriculum)

B. Extension of classwork (any more intensive or extensive study initiated by student or teacher of a subject in which the student is enrolled. e.g., extra credit work)

C. Independent project (the former definition still applies here)

1. The problem or topic need not be related to any academic field, but it should be performed under the guidance of a qualified adviser.

2. The student learns by designing and completing in a systematic and controlled manner a task he initiates and records in school files.

3. Because a student will probably do his best on a project if he does not feel it is just an assignment, he should engage in only one at a time unless he chooses to do more.
4. A student need not be confined to advisers from only one department but should be encouraged to seek help from anyone who is qualified.

D. Enrichment experiences

1. Movies ("Adventure Theater")
2. Library and resource centers
3. Class visitations
4. Specialty courses
5. Teacher-student conferences
6. Assistants to teachers and to resource center aides
7. Open labs

But this description came only after considerable experience. At first, after we had agreed to accept the earlier independent-study definition and after we had discussed our own attitudes and ideas, we outlined three major interests for the committee. We wanted to know what could be learned in independent study as we defined it, we wanted to know how we could motivate students to participate in an independent-study program, and we wanted to know how to evaluate a completed project. Initially we decided that the best justification for independent study, a justification which incidentally helps determine the teacher-adviser's role, was the organizational process the student would of necessity experience in independent study. Thus we established the acquisition of organizational skills as an important academic goal of the independent-study project.

We then tried various methods of attracting students to independent study. One teacher simply outlined our ideas to his students and asked them to begin projects. Another teacher told his students that a project was necessary for an A or B in English. Another substituted an independent project for a long assignment and graded each project as he would have the assignment.

But we all had one thing in common—we did not require that the project be related in any way to English, the subject we taught. The project was determined solely by the student's interest. All the methods worked. As one might expect, the teacher who graded each project got the greatest number of participants; the teacher who simply asked students to participate got the least. More important, however, the reactions of the students who had truly committed themselves to this project were encouragingly positive and were not related to the manner in which the teacher introduced independent study. We all thought we had learned a great deal from the experience.

One of the problems that arose during this first trial was the diversity of projects with which a given teacher might be confronted. The teacher who obtained the highest degree of participation was swamped with advisees and their projects. In order to cope with this problem, to help spread the idea of independent study, and to get new perspectives on the program, the committee was expanded to encompass representatives from most departments in the school. The expansion of the committee also facilitated communication among the departments and helped to encourage students in interdisciplinary projects.

STUDENT STRIDES

In the five years that independent study has been functioning at Marshall, student projects have ranged from fashion design to architecture and from lettering of poetry to musical composition. One of the most outstanding projects so far completed is a piano suite inspired by the moods of Crane's *The Red Badge of Courage*. This project is outstanding because it meets so well the goals we think independent study may achieve. The student made excellent use of his imaginative and inventive powers, and he subjected them to the most rigorous of organizational processes. In addition, he was able to find expression in one discipline for inspiration he received in another. Thus, for this student, independent study has helped not only in developing originality but in creating a more integrated view of experience.

Obviously, the student described could not have achieved what he did without the superior talents and skills he already possessed. But it was the independent-study program that prompted him to tap those talents as he did. Other students have achieved similar, though usually not such spectacular, results. A senior boy who normally reads and writes at about the sixth-grade level demonstrated a heat-powered engine which he had constructed from rough plans in a science magazine. The result here was much more far-reaching than the project itself. Because of the recognition he received for his project, the boy showed renewed interest in school, and his work in all subjects showed marked improvement. Incidentally, on graduation he received the only Dads' Club vocational-technical scholarship in his class. Two sophomore boys, also of limited academic ability, used real armor borrowed from a collector to produce a large-group presentation on medieval armor and warfare. Two senior girls, after thoroughly researching the subject of medieval scribes and manuscripts, lettered and illuminated the "General Prologue" to *The Canterbury Tales*. Another senior girl designed and constructed a whole wardrobe for her preschool niece, even though there is no instruction offered in children's clothing at Marshall. A freshman boy experimented with shrimp eggs to determine the factors affecting their success in hatching. Another freshman project, undertaken by a small group, was concerned with the history of the Portland area. This group worked through the summer with the Oregon Historical Society and others to find as many little-known historical remnants of early Oregon as they could. This project developed into an enrichment, or prerogative, course (a noncredit course established at the prerogative of the teachers and students for varying lengths of time), which the group continued during their sophomore year. These are just a few projects from a tremendously varied assortment.

Not all projects are as good or as obviously worthwhile as these, of course. A junior boy submitted a painting that looked remarkably like colored worms squirming on the canvas. This strange effect was not so mysterious after the boy explained that he had achieved it by dipping worms in paint and letting them crawl randomly across the canvas. His adviser agreed that the technique was original, but indicated he felt the worms had been more creative than the artist. The boy's second project, a movie he produced on the wildlife and scenery of the Columbia River Gorge, was finished in May, 1966; like most second tries in independent-study projects, it was a much more satisfying achievement for all concerned.

It is probably clear from the descriptions and comments above that one of the significant problems in our independent-study program is motivation and follow-up. The problem of motivation is complex. We want students to be self-motivated, yet we want them to know we expect them to do their best. Although a student's achievement in independent study necessarily influences his teachers when they are awarding report-card grades, most of us no longer formally relate independent study to subject grades. If a project is graded, it appears to be just another assignment and is treated as such. Instead we try to find ways of discovering student interests and channeling them into some kind of productive activity without making a formal assignment. Many teachers use small-group discussions for this purpose. They ask students to discuss with each other the kinds of things they have found interesting in the past and then capitalize on the individual's interest in his own experiences. Many teachers bring examples of student projects to demonstrate the range of endeavor open to all. But when a student has decided on an area in which he is interested and has chosen an adviser, the teacher's job has just begun. The adviser must help limit and define the subject so that the student is able to determine the project or activity he can complete. Essential at this point and in the completion of the project is the individual conference. One teacher may stimulate a student to begin a project; the student may choose as his adviser a teacher he never meets in class. Since many students need frequent encouragement to complete a project successfully, the conference is almost requisite to success.

The best results have been obtained when the student has outlined his project, established a conference schedule, and committed himself to completing some part of the project by each conference. To help facilitate these conference schedules and to make available the information on student projects, the Independent Study Committee devised a project description form for schoolwide use. (See Figure 4–1.) One copy of the form is placed in a central file open to all teachers. Here the school has a permanent record of all independent projects, here counselors may find valuable information on student ability and interests, and here independent study finds a concrete basis for schoolwide interdepartmental growth. Thus the implementation of the independent-study description form and the increasing use of the individual conference for independent study are valuable tools in establishing the kind of motivation we think necessary for the success of our program.

Another difficult aspect of the independent-study project is the problem of evaluation. At first many of us found it almost insurmountable, but after working with a number of students on various kinds of projects, most of us have decided not to evaluate projects formally. The description form requires that the student meet with his adviser and that the adviser make appropriate comments about the project. Since most teachers in the school are now interested in independent study, it is usually easy to find an adviser who has some familiarity with the student's subject. Also, the Independent Study Committee has developed publicity channels which help focus student-body attention on independent study. As a result of all these factors, the students are becoming more self-critical and more able to evaluate their own work. We have found that evaluation by others, especially by teachers, is a motivating force secondary to the emphasis we have placed on personal pride and accomplishment.

TOWARD INDEPENDENT HEALTH

Our efforts thus far in independent study have been to make our school a place in which the student may find acceptance and recognition for his constructive approaches to self-expression. We want to establish a climate in which such expression is afforded the highest honors. We still have many problems to overcome before we reach that climate. We have not yet

Independent Study Record
John Marshall High School

______________________________ 9 10 11 12

Last name First name

Subject:

Topic: (Subject narrowed down to a workable thesis)

Adviser ____________________ Date approved __________

Brief description of project: Proposed due date __________

____

____

____

____

____

____

____

____

____

Conferences:

______ ______________________________
Date

______ ______________________________
Date

______ ______________________________
Date

______ ______________________________
Date

______ ______________________________
Date

FIGURE 4-1

actively engaged all the faculty in independent study, nor have we yet succeeded in giving real academic weight to all worthy independent projects. Also we have not yet fully developed the kind and degree of publicity for independent study which we would like. Consequently, we have yet to convince many of our students that the school places the highest values on independent study.

But these are some of the goals toward which we are working, some of the specific problems which the Independent Study Committee originally intended to consider. We have made real progress. We have a majority of the faculty and students, students from all grade and ability levels, participating in independent study. Mathematics and industrial arts teachers are advising students on projects which originated in English classes and for which students receive recognition from teachers in several classes. English teachers are helping students to organize written work on science and social studies projects. We have developed a central filing system and a description form which make accessible to the entire school information on independent study. We have a display case in which projects are frequently featured, and we have a school newspaper column devoted to independent study. Independent study is clearly an important part of the Marshall community.

There are many reasons to hope and to believe that in the near future the great majority of Marshall students will find the climate which will help them to grow into responsible self-motivated citizens, citizens who will feel that their contribution to their community is important. For many of these students, the teachers of Marshall will have made much of this growth possible through their recognition of personal interests and independent achievement. Admittedly, independent study is only beginning here even after several years of pioneering this concept, but the freedom and enthusiasm it has already generated in both students and faculty make the propects for the future appear sunny indeed.

5

Independent Study: Enrichment Experiences

Lyle K. Meyer

Independent study is a curious animal: Much like the fable of the blind men describing the elephant, there is a danger in trying to explain independent study in isolated segments rather than considering it in light of a total educational environment. Not convinced that the traditional method of scheduling was the most effective way for them to teach or for their students to learn, the staff at Marshall High School made the decision to pioneer a computer-generated flexible scheduling program. The advent of flexible scheduling dismissed both the traditional study hall and the conventional method of scheduling seven periods of equal length for each school day. Flexible scheduling allows the teachers sufficient time to meet in teams for planning sessions and to confer with students individually and in small groups. It also provides the students at Marshall with a unique opportunity to individualize their learning. Students are able to determine for themselves how their unscheduled time should be used. Thus, one of the faculty's primary objectives is to concentrate on improving the opportunities for independent study. By assisting the students in making constructive use of their unscheduled time, we enable them to utilize the facilities and personnel available to them.

A WORKING DEFINITION

A description of independent study can be suggested by saying that independent-study *time* refers to those modules a student is not scheduled into a class for which he receives credit (approximately 40 percent of a student's program). *Independent study* refers to the student's constructive use of his unscheduled time.

Proceeding with our working definition that independent study will mean the constructive use of unscheduled time, we can describe the four basic activities in which a student may participate during this time. First, a student often does his regularly assigned classwork; second, the student may become involved in an extensive or intensive extension of his regular class assignment—more likely than not, a student would be given "extra credit" for this type of work; third, a student might be engaged in an independent-study project, a discussion of which immediately precedes this chapter; finally, a student could participate in an enrichment experience. Although the term "enrichment experience" seems a bit unwieldy for a description, it is an appropriate one, for it does suggest the nature of the activity. It is the purpose of this chapter to consider some of the variety of activities that are described as enrichment experiences, experiences that for the most part a student would not have encountered if Marshall High School were still on a conventional scheduling system.

Although a student is often engaged in a variety of activities during his unscheduled, independent-study time—he may study in the library or any one of the seven resource centers, confer with teachers or his fellow students, practice on a musical instrument, work on an independent-study project, listen and respond to language tapes—there is a good possibility that he may include an enrichment experience. Enrichment experiences include an array of specialty courses, unique training activities, class auditing on a formal or informal basis, and special programs that are available to the students because of the flexibility of our scheduling system.

A SERIES OF POSSIBILITIES

Among the many enrichment experiences offered to students during one school year under our modular-flexible design were the following specialty courses, training activities, and special programs:

1. Slide-rule class
2. Creative writing
3. Knitting instruction
4. Conversational Japanese
5. Greek instruction
6. Oil painting
7. Clothing construction
8. Italic lettering
9. Weight lifting
10. Clarinet instruction
11. Creativity class
12. Charm course
13. Dance band
14. Literature class
15. Lab technician course
16. Drama festival
17. Automotive program
18. Adventure Theatre
19. Office assistant program
20. Librarian's book review committee

This list, of course, is not all-inclusive, but it does serve to illustrate the variety of enrichment experiences offered to the students. Several of these activities have been available for more than one year, and many of them are repeated each year. The "teacher-assistant" program is a flourishing one, inaugurated during the third year of our new design, and has proved exceedingly worthwhile for both students and teachers.

SPECIALTY COURSES

The specialty or prerogative course was an interesting and unforeseen development. Inasmuch as teachers have unscheduled time during the week, they are able to offer such courses to interested students. The specialty course offers neither credit nor grade. A student enrolls for the best of reasons: He is interested in the subject and wants to learn. And teachers teach the courses for similar reasons: They have a special interest in the subject, and they enjoy teaching interested students.

It is difficult to describe the specialty courses as a whole in specific terms, for by their very nature, the courses are specialized and individual. The courses are a supplement to, rather than a part of, the official school curriculum. And the courses do not follow a rigid pattern of, say, fifteen students enrolled for nine weeks meeting twice each week for one hour. The courses are offered by any teacher who has an inclination to teach such a course, and with few exceptions, the courses are offered without prerequisites to any student who expresses an interest in attending the class meetings. Thus, the courses generally operate on a completely ungraded basis. The classes meet before, during, and after school. The determining factor is one of mutual convenience. If the teacher and the student find that a sufficient number of unscheduled modules correspond on their respective programs, the course may be offered during regular school hours. Some teachers find it more convenient to schedule the classes immediately after school; still others have found it most satisfactory to schedule the class before the school day officially begins.

The courses that have been taught are as varied as the interests and personalities of the teachers involved. To suggest the scope, classes have been offered in the areas of music, industrial arts, physical education, home economics, English, art, foreign language, and mathematics. Thus during the 1965–1966 school year, courses were offered in subjects as diverse as clarinet instruction, taught by a business education teacher; Greek instruction, taught by a speech instructor; conversational Japanese, taught by a science teacher; and instrumental music, taught by a mathematics teacher.

The dangers inherent in generalizing about specific courses are obvious. Since an "average" specialty course does not exist, because of their diverse characteristics, a more satisfactory way to consider the nature and function of the specialty courses would be to describe a few of those that have been taught.

Although basic and advanced courses are offered in Russian, Spanish, German, French, and Latin, the foreign language department is not able to offer instruction in Greek. The number of students who indicate an interest in learning Greek is, understandably, quite limited. In the traditionally scheduled program, no provision was apparent for the exceptional youngster who might want to learn Greek.

In the fall of 1964, two students learned that one of Marshall's speech teachers spoke Greek fluently. They asked if he would tutor them, and the wheels were quickly set in motion. As a matter of fact, the wheels continue to move today, for the class has increased in size from two students to six, including one English teacher!

The classes were scheduled for one hour twice a week during school time, at such a time when all members of the class had corresponding unscheduled modules. During the second year the class met, a second instructor was added. The students met in class with the speech teacher at Marshall during the week and attended special meetings on Saturdays at a neighborhood church, where they were taught by a native of Greece.

How many high school curricula include Japanese as a course available to the student? Few do, I am sure. Yet such a course was offered at Marshall. This course was taught not by a multilingual whiz in the foreign language department, but by a secretary in the counseling department and a science teacher. The history of the course seems worth relating.

The first all-school play presented during the 1965–1966 school year was *Teahouse of the August Moon.* The cast for the play includes a Japanese houseboy, and it was necessary for the student cast for this part to speak a number of Japanese words and phrases. The drama teacher made inquiries and learned that the counseling department secretary and a science teacher spoke Japanese. They agreed to assist the student with the correct diction and pronunciation necessary for the part. The student playing the role of the Japanese houseboy did a creditable job, and the play was a success. The story, however, does not end at this point.

Some time after the play had been presented, a junior girl decided she would like to have a fundamental knowledge of her parents' native language, Japanese. She was directed to the science teacher, who agreed to tutor her for the balance of the year. They met in the science teacher's office during independent-study time on a regularly scheduled program. The science department chairman soon learned of his colleague's tutoring activities and suggested she expand her efforts. She then placed an announcement in the morning bulletin indicating that she would be available to teach the fundamentals of conversational Japanese to interested students. Several students responded to her invitation, and after she had explained the nature of the course in detail, five students elected to enroll in the course. (Incidentally, the eleventh-grade student who previously was being tutored by the science instructor joined this specialty class, although she also continued to be tutored as previously planned throughout the year.) The five students continued in the course from the time the course started, in January, until the end of the school year.

This specialty course, like most, was an ungraded one and included members of the sophomore, junior, and senior classes. The students ended the course in an appropriate fashion; they had a Japanese dinner and evidenced their proficiency at chopsticks throughout the dinner, even to the extent of eating an American dessert, Jello, with their Japanese utensils.

In another example a two-member team from the science department decided to offer a specialty course for one primary reason: They believed they could give a number of students sufficient training to obtain summer positions as assistants to lab technicians in a medical laboratory or hospital. They felt that a student could be sufficiently trained in the techniques of preparing solutions, sterilizing lab equipment, and assisting in the collection of routine test data to enable the student to obtain a temporary summer job and, in addition, to provide a basic background for any of the students who might want to continue study after graduation to become a registered lab technician. (*Note:* Both of the teachers who taught this course are registered lab technicians in addition to being fully accredited science teachers.)

The teachers announced to their large-group biology class that they would be willing to teach the course if interest was indicated by enough students to warrant the training program. Thirty-four of the students indicated an initial interest. After the plans for the course were detailed, ten students officially enrolled. This ungraded specialty course, taught throughout by the science team, was designed for a ten-week period, including regular instruction during independent-study time, assignments to be completed during the student's unscheduled time, and a field trip to a local biological supply company. Of the ten students who originally signed up for the course, nine completed it and the other student transferred to another school after the course was started.

The teachers and students alike were enthusiastic about the results; consequently, this two-teacher team hopes to continue this activity each year. If time allows, they will instruct their students in the procedures of blood typing and blood counts, as they have the necessary lab equipment at their disposal. The instructors indicated that the only real limiting factor in the course was that of time. This is certainly understandable, for a specialty course such as they taught requires a considerable amount of preparation.

A member of the home economics department initiated a specialty course at the request of several of her students. Knitting instruction is not included in the regular home economics curriculum, and so the students asked the teacher if she would teach a specialty course on the fundamentals of knitting. Thirty-three girls attended the first meeting of the class, at which time the teacher discussed with them the possibilities of the course. It was agreed that the students would meet for one hour per week during their independent-study time until they felt they had gained a sufficient mastery of the fundamental skills. The students were free to "drop" the course at any time they so desired. Since a sincere interest for learning was the only requirement for enrolling in the course, the class included students from every grade level. As a corollary note, the heterogeneous nature of this ungraded class is reflected by the grade-point averages of the students in the class; they ranged from 1.8 (D+) to 3.83 (A).

Another interesting feature about this specialty course is the fact that the home economics teacher is no longer the only instructor. The mother of one of the girls in the class is the sponsor of a local 4-H Club. She was asked to help chaperon when the group visited one of the local knitting mills. Her interest in the program piqued, the mother contacted the teacher to see if she could be of any assistance in helping the girls in their classwork. As a result the knitting course is now taught by two instructors—an unusual but very successful team-teaching operation.

One final note is appropriate. The mother who assisted in the instruction encouraged several interested girls to join the 4-H Club. In the spring of 1966, three of these girls applied for and received 4-H Club scholarships to attend a summer workshop at Oregon State University to learn about the latest developments in the area of home economics. This course was offered again the following year. The only change was to limit its length. It is now designed for an eight- to ten-week period to allow more students to participate.

A luncheon conversation with the instrumental music teacher was the starting point for a specialty course in clarinet instruction. One of the business education teachers at Marshall minored in music in college and has maintained an active interest in music over the years. Inasmuch as his particular musical talent is playing the clarinet, he offered to assist the students who played the clarinet and who were also enrolled in an instrumental music course. The result was 8 one-hour-long meetings over a period of several weeks. During this time the teacher met with the students giving individual instructions as well as working with several quartet groups. The students met with the teacher during common independent-study modules in the music room.

"One man's work is another man's hobby" may be a rather tired cliché, but it is a truism in action in at least one situation at Marshall. One of our teachers, although a full-time member of the mathematics department, has an extensive background in music and has often performed with professional groups. For the past three years he has met with fifteen to twenty students from 7:15 to 8:00 A.M. at least twice a week. The group is officially recognized as Marshall's dance band and is often asked to perform at special assemblies and for school dances. The only requirement for enrollment in this specialty class is that the student be enrolled in the regular instrumental music program at school, and even this requirement has been waived in several instances.

Instruction concerning the basic functions and manipulations of the slide rule was the basis for yet another specialty course. Twelve interested math students asked their instructor if he would be willing to teach the course, and with his consent the class was started. Because of a number of conflicts in their schedules—that is, their independent-study modules did not correspond—the class met at 7:30 on Monday and Wednesday mornings for a period of six weeks. The instructor indicated the students successfully accomplished their objective, and the course is being offered again this year.

THE QUESTION OF PUBLICITY

Announcement of special events for students during their independent-study time is made in a variety of ways. Whether it be a guest speaker for a large group, a short- or long-term specialty course, a field trip, a dramatic production, or a film of special interest, the instructor may put an announcement in the daily bulletin to be read in each registration room in the morning, place an announcement in the appropriate resource center, display a poster in a display window in the main hall, or place an announcement card on one of the announcement boards in the main hall. The two special announcement boards were built specifically for publicizing individual independent-study activities and enrichment experiences available to students. The announcement boards are attractively designed, glass-enclosed, rectangular cases measuring 6 by 3 feet each. Incidentally, this project was an activity of the school's independent-study committee with funds made available by the Dads' Club.

When a teacher is teaching a specialty course or has a guest speaker coming for a large group, for example, he simply opens the window covering the announcement board and places a card on the appropriate modules. There is sufficient room on the card to indicate the subject, teacher, room, and any other pertinent data.

A rather unusual enrichment experience was offered to interested industrial arts students in the spring of 1966. Although Marshall offers both basic and advanced industrial arts courses, in the area of wood, metal, drafting, and electronics, there are no facilities at present for an automotive shop. Thus, the automotive program, cosponsored by a physics and an electronics teacher, constituted a unique opportunity for Marshall's students.

The program was planned to offer students some formal experience relating to the automotive industry. A survey was conducted to determine student interest in the program, and 140 students attended the initial meeting when the objectives of the program were outlined. Students would have a chance to learn more about the automotive industry by seeing films, observing demonstrations, going on field trips, listening to guest speakers and, it was hoped, by actively participating to some degree by demonstrating the practical application of what they had learned about tuning a car's engine.

After the organizational meetings were complete, the students went on a field trip during their independent-study time to observe the newest automotive diagnostic equipment. (Because of the number of interested students, two trips had to be scheduled.) Next, a guest speaker from a local automotive firm was invited to come to school and demonstrate specific timing apparatus. At this time a complete demonstration employing an engine simulator was provided for the students.

Although this activity was met with enthusiasm and the instructors were very pleased by the number of students who participated in the program, the very size of the group necessitated the restriction of one part of the proposed plan, that of having the students work on their own cars to demonstrate what they had learned about tuning engines. During the 1966–1967 school year the program was refined so that more students could be served with fewer in each group. Modifications of the original program resulted in a series of five-week specialty courses which accommodated all students interested in this elementary but practical automotive training.

A DRAMATIC EXPERIENCE

With flexible scheduling, many things may be accomplished in the drama department that cannot be done under a traditional program, because of the availability of students during the school day. The drama program in most secondary schools follows one of two directions: Either it is limited to those students regularly enrolled in drama classes, with rehearsals scheduled during the day, or the main stage (all-school) productions are rehearsed after school, allowing all interested students to participate. Most schools prefer the latter method. Flexible scheduling allows the drama teacher to schedule students who are not officially enrolled in drama into several drama classes during the week. Thus the student who, because of a job commitment, a heavy academic load, or a scheduling conflict, is not able to take drama as one of his official courses is still given every opportunity to participate in the drama program during his independent-study time.

A vivid example of the enrichment experiences available to students is the Theater Arts Festival, a series of plays offered by the drama department in the spring of 1966. A primary objective of the festival was to expose as many students as possible to live drama, both as participants and as spectators. The plays selected for the festival were representative productions from the nineteenth and twentieth centuries. A total of fifteen plays were presented thirty-seven times. Of the fifteen plays, nine were one-act plays, three were one-act excerpts from three-act plays, and three were full-length children's theater productions. Each production was presented at least twice before live audiences.

Students enrolled in the drama classes for credit rehearsed during their regularly scheduled small-group meetings. The fifty students who performed in the plays and who were not officially enrolled in the drama classes were scheduled into the small-group meetings during their independent-study time. After several weeks of rehearsals, each group held an after-school dress rehearsal.

Although the drama teacher directed all fifteen of the productions, each of the fifteen small groups was responsible for designing and building their own sets and designing and constructing their own costumes. The students enrolled in drama for credit were placed in positions of responsibility and were given every opportunity to practice what they had learned by assisting the fifty students who participated in the festival but who were not enrolled in the regular drama classes. (It is interesting to note that all the "extra" fifty students who participated in the festival were cast in acting roles.)

Twelve of the fifteen plays were presented at Marshall. They were given in large-group English classes to all grade and ability levels. It is estimated that 2,000 of Marshall's 2,200 students saw at least one of the plays. The three plays not presented at Marshall were hour-long children's theater productions (*Pinocchio, Puss in Boots,* and *The Farmer and the Fox*). These plays, arranged with the cooperation of the principals involved, were presented at all-school assemblies (grades one through eight) at four of the eight elementary schools which contribute to the Marshall student body. Approximately 2,400 grade-school students enjoyed the performances.

Altogether, nearly 170 students took an active part in the Theater Arts Festival. The plays were very well received, both at the high school and the elementary schools. The fact that some 4,400 students viewed the plays is sufficient testimony to the success of the festival, a memorable enrichment experience for participants and audience alike.

A different type of enrichment activity involved the use of students as assistants to resource-center aides. Members of the Marshall FTA club (Future Teachers of America) were invited to attend a meeting one afternoon in the English resource center. At that time a training program for resource-center assistants was explained to them by a member of the English department and the English resource-center aide. Interested students from the FTA group would serve on a voluntary basis in the English resource center and would be taught the necessary skills to become resource-center assistants. They would learn book check-out procedures, help students looking for specific information, assist in the inventory checks at the end of the school year, correct objective tests, and do occasional typing and clerical assignments for teachers in the English department. After the proposal had been explained to them, many of the club members expressed an interest in participating in the training program. The students indicated the independent-study modules they would be able to work without interfering with their school work, and this information was given to the resource-center aide, who compiled a schedule whereby the students would come in at regularly scheduled modules throughout the week. The aide would then work with the students on a one-to-one basis until the training period was completed.

Though the students did not receive formal academic credit for this training, it was a very successful program. Of the eleven students who expressed an interest at the original meeting, nine completed their training; the students served an average of 120 modules each, with a few students totaling over 200 modules. Indeed, a few of the assistants became so interested in their work that they volunteered to serve as assistants in the library in addition to their work in the English resource center.

TOTALING THE FIGURES

When visitors to Marshall are told that approximately one-third of the students enrolled are not in class during any single module of the day, their reaction is oftentimes one of surprise. And the question, "What do the students do during this time?" is to be expected. As indicated earlier in this chapter, the student on independent-study time has a considerable number of opportunities available to him. He may, of course, go to the library or any one of the several resource centers. He could have a conference with one of the instructors simply by checking the conference modules on his teacher's program (each teacher's schedule is posted in alphabetical order in the main hall). Then again, the student might go to one of the many open-lab areas maintained in industrial arts, business education, chemistry, physics, reading, foreign language, home economics, art, and science classrooms. Certainly, the student who uses his time in a judicious manner has no lack of educational resources at his disposal.

But do the students utilize the facilities offered to them? The answer is a resounding "yes." Several times since Marshall has been on its modular-flexible program, checks have been made to ascertain the use of the facilities available to the students. In order to obtain a meaningful attendance survey, a daily modular tally was recorded by the clerks, aides, and librarians for each day of *a* week for a period of five weeks. According to the compiled statistics, the library and resource centers were utilized to the following degree:

Resource center	*Capacity*	*Attendance*
English–social studies (ninth grade)	67	3,871
Mathematics	43	1,108
Science	32	1,515
Social studies	75	3,559
Art, home economics, industrial arts, P.E.	45	2,847
English	81	4,032
Business education	33	1,294
Library	175	12,350
		30,576

This attendance count represents the sum total of students in the library and resource centers during each module of the day for a one-week period. It does not, of course, reflect students in open-lab classes in foreign language, science, music, reading, art, etc.

Perhaps a more inclusive study of student activity during unscheduled time is revealed by a carefully conducted statistical study during the fourth year of the program, which indicated that in any given module of approximately 660 students on independent time, 385 will be in the resource centers and library; 95 taking a "break" in the student union; and 180 in open labs, individual teacher or counselor conferences, or auditing classes.

Though our successes at Marshall are considerable and the opportunities for students impressive, we still have problems before us. Perhaps the most persistent problem confronting the faculty is that of the small percentage of students who do not use their independent-study time wisely. With a solution to this problem in mind Marshall High School applied for and received a grant from the Kettering Foundation. The study is identifying the type of students who are not effective in independent study and is providing a program to help those students become effective and responsible in their use of independent-study time. The final report of this study will be available in September, 1968, and should be of significant assistance to schools moving into a flexible instructional design.

After five years of pioneering independent study, we feel that we have a considerable way to go in order to realize the full potential inherent in this new concept in secondary education. There is little doubt in the minds of most of us that the key to individualizing teaching and learning, and the key to a successful modular-flexible design, is in the implementation of a dynamic, creative, and intense independent-study program. The staff at Marshall High School intends to do just that as we continue to develop and refine our total program.

6

Resource Centers and the Instructional Materials Center

William R. Gray, Jr.

The Marshall modular design allows the student to spend approximately one-third or more of his time in unstructured independent educational pursuits. It is important to note that *all* students at Marshall are scheduled with independent-study time. This means that during any one module, approximately one-third of the student body has unstructured time available for a variety of independent-study activities. As the program is based on a weekly cycle, no two days within a week are identical; thus, some days offer students more unstructured time than others. It is, of course, imperative to have both facilities and learning materials available for students if unstructured time is to become a part of the program, and these facilities and materials must be adequate for a large part of the student body at any given time. Consequently, we have provided our students with a variety of areas in which they may choose to do their work: seven subject resource centers; a communications laboratory; the main library; open laboratories in science, shops, art, home economics, business education, language, mathematics, and music. The student may also confer individually with a teacher in his office or keep an appointment with his counselor in the counseling suite. He may choose to take a break in the student union, which is available throughout the day. Because of the available time that each student has for independent study, it is important that as many resource areas as possible be available to him.

THE RESOURCE-CENTER DESIGN

This new program presented Marshall's librarian, the department chairmen, and the administrative staff with the problem of developing a library system that would expand and extend throughout the school building and provide adequate physical facilities, materials, and supervision for students during their unscheduled time.

It was necessary that this extension of the library be much more than supervised study halls. It was conspicuously apparent that additional professional and paraprofessional personnel had to be added to the library staff so that the program could get off the ground with an organized resource-center system that would provide adequate physical facilities as well as adequate learning materials.

The resource center, as defined by our staff, is an area containing materials and equipment needed by students to pursue their learning during their independent-study time in a specific discipline, or in two or more disciplines. Besides the artifacts needed for the specific subject, resource centers provide a teacher aide to assist students in locating appropriate materials and also at times is staffed by teachers who work directly with students requiring professional assistance. Although a part of the instructional materials department, headed by the librarian, the resource center is an integral part of the organization of the subject-matter departments, and this is controlled in large measure by the department chairman and his staff. (See Organizational Chart, Figure 6–1.)

The aims and goals in the implementation of the instructional materials center and resource-center plan at Marshall High School are essentially the aims of the Portland public schools

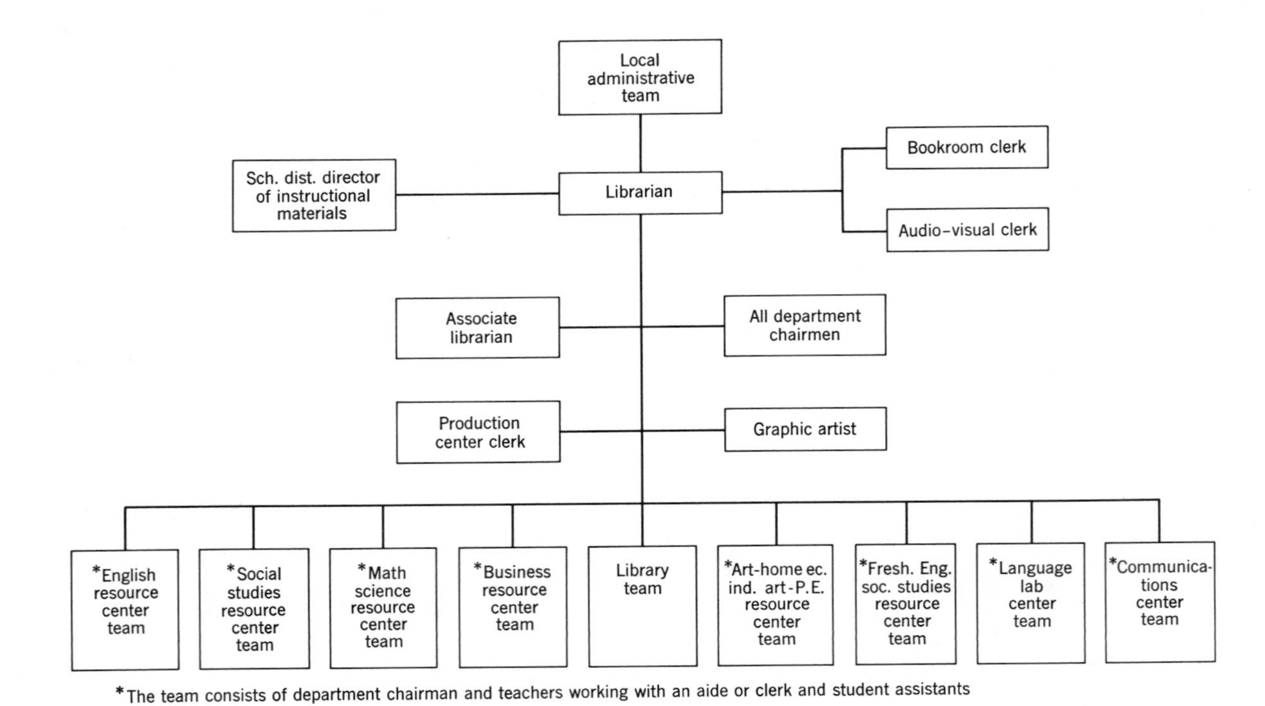

*The team consists of department chairman and teachers working with an aide or clerk and student assistants

FIGURE 6-1. Instructional materials department and resource-center organizational chart

instructional-materials-center concept. This farsighted policy states:

> The instructional materials center supports the total school program by acquiring many kinds of materials to meet the curricular and personal needs of *all* students, as well as by providing guidance in their use. It helps to develop in students habits and skills of independent investigation so that they can use libraries, whether public, high school, college or university with profit and pleasure. It provides opportunities for students to expand their interests and to acquire desirable social attitudes. It encourages the development of lifelong habits in the pursuit of knowledge, not only through the printed page but also through the newer media of communication by which students are daily surrounded.

This philosophy, as outlined by district policy, was used as a guideline to implement the resource-center concept that would be part of a reorganized instructional materials center under the direct supervision of the librarian. Modest outside funding enabled us to further develop the spirit of this philosophy.

The thinking that went into planning the resource centers the year previous to the implementation of the new program included ideas from the entire staff of the school. Each department met with the librarian to establish some immediate and long-range goals for resource centers. These ideas varied from department to department. It is interesting to note how quickly after implementation we were moving into areas we had not foreseen or previously discussed. It is not possible to foresee all the ramifications or necessary adjustments to implement a resource-center program in a school. Once started, adjustments can be made easily; moreover, they are more realistic and appropriate after the initial implementation experience.

Teachers are the key to student use of the resource centers. Moreover, there must be adjustments in the traditional teaching assignment patterns if the available advantage of resource centers is used in broadening the resources and research materials that are available for students. Records, tapes, filmstrips, and a variety of supplementary materials must be readily available as well as assistance in using these resources.

The resource center "zeros in" on the needs of a department in the areas of instructional materials, supervised independent study, conference areas for teachers, meeting room for committees working on projects, and other teacher- or student-initiated activities. Therefore, resource centers at Marshall were designed by the teachers under the leadership of the department chairmen, the librarian, the associate librarian, and the administrative staff.

The equipment, physical facilities, textbooks, and supplementary materials for the instructional materials center and resource centers were necessarily the immediate concern of our staff. With the assistance and consultation of the director of instructional materials and the assistant superintendent for instruction of the Portland School District, district funds were utilized to secure appropriate materials for the centers. Additional supplementary and library budgets enabled us to add approximately $20,000 in library books to our rather small collection of 10,000 volumes. As a new school, we were in the process of building our collections. This additional support enabled the library to increase its holdings to about 15,000 volumes, and an additional 8,000 volumes went to the resource centers. At the end of the fourth year in the new design, the combined holdings of the library and resource centers accumulated to about 38,000 volumes, with about 20,000 in the main library. Although we continue to add diversified materials as needed and as funds are available, the growth in total amount of materials since the fourth year has been relatively limited.

The excellent collection in the resource centers was established without any real strain on the main library collection. We have been able to duplicate materials for the main library and resource center; however, there has been a problem in trying to keep up with the cataloging of the materials for centers. The materials in some of the centers are still in the process of being cataloged. Personnel in the resource centers that have completed this cataloging are now facing the problem of finding the time to develop bibliographies of instructional materials on units being taught in the classroom. This material for teachers and students is one of the keys to our independent-study program. It is a team effort on the part of the associate librarian, the audio-visual clerk, and the aides in the resource centers to continue to work with teachers on the use of this material in their curricula.

One other problem that required teacher and administrative planning was changing the procedure of classroom-rotating sets of textbooks in English to a textbook for every student member of the English large group. This large group might include one-half of the freshman, sophomore, junior, or senior students. Because of budget problems, it required that the team select paperback editions whenever possible, so that every member of the class might have a copy. The paperback editions were able to provide the necessary materials to fill this gap, as most of the district's adopted texts are published in this form.

THE PARAPROFESSIONAL

With initial financial support from the Oregon Program, Marshall High School was able to secure clerical and teacher-aide assistance for teachers. The selection of this personnel was the responsibility of the department chairmen and the curriculum vice-principal working with excellent cooperation from the personnel department of the Portland public schools.

Resource-center aides were selected according to training and interest areas. Some of the aides were certified teachers in the subject served by the resource center, although their salaries are approximately one-half that of a teacher. Others had some college training with a strong interest in a subject area. All were interested in teaching library skills to young people. The paraprofessional is a member of the department team and is asked to assume some of the clerical duties normally performed by teachers, thereby enabling the teacher to have more school time for lesson preparation, team planning, and additional student conferences.

Paraprofessionals were selected for the following resource centers:

1. English resource center—sophomore, junior, and senior English students.

2. English and social studies resource center—freshman students.
3. Science resource center—all science students.
4. Math resource center—all math students.
5. Industrial arts, art, home economics, physical education and health resource center—for all students in these departments.
6. Business education resource center—all business students.
7. Social studies resource center—sophomore, junior, and senior students.
8. Language lab—The aide works with language teachers in the development of the language lab. This position was later designated as a language-lab technician. All language students use this lab.
9. Communications lab—A professional teacher was assigned the task of developing a communications lab and general reading-improvement program.

Three clerical assistants were also hired to assist teachers in the production work in large departments. The English department, with eighteen teachers, needed extra clerical assistance. The social studies department required clerical assistance in adapting the traditional curriculum to the new modes of learning —large group and small group. The freshman English and social studies teachers needed clerical assistance for the additional production work, and this clerk was also assigned any overflow production work that needed to be done in other departments.

The general duties of the resource-center aides differ to some degree in each resource center, but they have been generalized as follows:

1. Supervising resource center; helping students find materials and aiding them with independent-study problems
2. Acting as liaison between administration office and teachers and between teachers and students
3. Checking out materials
4. Assisting teachers in the classroom

5. Taking roll in the large group; recording absences and cuts in master file
6. Making bibliographies and searching in magazines and newspapers for resource materials
7. Organizing files
8. Grading and recording tests; administering make-up tests
9. Organizing bulletin-board displays
10. Typing materials for teachers
11. Checking in the textbooks of students withdrawing from school

The list of duties of department clerks is generalized as follows:

1. Open the resource center at 8:00 A.M. for student use; check in "overnight" books; straighten bookshelves.
2. Type material: tests, study guides, outlines for all teachers; use mimeograph and ditto machines properly; assemble work promptly for teachers.
3. Take roll in large group and assist in keeping attendance records.
4. Help grade objective tests and mark IBM grade cards when necessary.
5. Make cards for books in resource center.
6. Sort through magazines and newspapers for suitable material for files.
7. Help put up bulletin-board displays.
8. Type business letters for teachers (requesting material, etc.).
9. Relieve aide in resource center for lunch, breaks, etc.

ADMINISTRATIVE POLICY FOR RESOURCE CENTERS

Once the idea of centers had been established and aides had been selected to administer them, it was necessary to develop some policy for administration. Listed below are the early policies as developed by the librarian, the associate librarian, department chairmen, and aides:

1. The primary purpose of the aide on duty in the resource center is to be of assistance to the students in finding materials for their use.
2. The secondary purpose of the aide is to assist the teachers in the distribution and collection of assignments, projects, worksheets, etc., and other tasks for which time is available. (This will vary with individual departments.)
3. The aide maintains discipline, keeps the room neat and attractive, keeps materials orderly and available, and creates a quiet atmosphere in which students can study effectively.
4. The aide will work in close cooperation with the instructional materials director (librarian), the associate director (associate librarian), and the department chairman to ensure efficient operation of the center.
5. Generally, materials are not to be checked out of resource centers. (This may vary, however, according to circumstances and the needs of the individual departments.)
6. As a general policy, students are not to leave resource centers during the module.
7. The materials in the resource centers should be handled according to the procedures established at meetings with IMD, associate IMD, department chairmen, and aides and clerks. Procedures will vary somewhat with the individual center.
8. The aides and clerks are responsible for maintaining attractive, informative, and useful bulletin boards. Materials should be obtained from teachers, IMD, associate IMD. It is advisable to have teachers give aides and clerks the lesson assignments far enough in advance so that materials can be obtained by the IMD and associate IMD for the resource centers.
9. The aide having problems with students or teachers in the resource center should feel free to discuss them with the

IMD, the associate IMD, the department chairman or to bring them up at meetings.

10. Supplies are obtained through the book room. Mechanical failures of typewriters should be reported to the head secretary. Any difficulty with audio-visuals should be reported.
11. Official notice will be given to the aides when the resource centers are to be closed.
12. If students are disorderly and the aide is unable to handle the situation, she should take the students' names, send them to the administrative vice-principal, and call on the intercom to notify the office.
13. A student who has been absent may obtain assignments that are past due from the resource center.

It was felt that students should have minimal guidelines for proper use of the centers; consequently, a set of student responsibilities in resource centers was developed. From time to time these policies are modified. At present they state:

1. Resource-center hours are 8:00 A.M. to 4:00 P.M.
2. On independent-study time, a student may enter or leave the center only at the passing time.
3. Students do not leave the resource center during the module for any reason without special permission from the person in charge.
4. Students are responsible for having needed books, materials, etc., with them when they enter the center.
5. Students may study, do reference work, use audio and visual aids, or do leisure reading in the resource center.
6. Students may obtain late assignments from the resource-center aide.
7. Library-type conduct must be maintained in the centers at all times.

THE STUDENT AND THE RESOURCE CENTER

From the student's point of view, an opportunity to use the resources of the school during the school day is a "great idea." As one senior student put it, "It gives me an opportunity to participate in sports and family activities without the constant pressure of homework." Certainly, this plan does not completely eliminate homework for the students; however, it does remove a considerable amount of pressure and gives those students who find it necessary to work on an outside job or those students who are active in community youth activities an opportunity to complete the majority of school work at school. By providing well-lighted and comfortable centers with an appealing atmosphere, the school is assisting in the development of good study habits and study-attack skills which are needed to assist students in their academic development.

To expose the student to opportunities for developing his potential today in education is as important as the three R's were yesterday. The growing complexity of our society demands that the accelerated students and the slow learners be given the opportunity to be awakened, stimulated, and provoked into a comfortable familiarity with a variety of learning materials, according to their particular needs, interests, and capabilities. Having these materials at his very fingertips in an attractive and pleasing living-room-type arrangement can help to develop the proper attitudes for all students.

An important feature of the resource center is simply that it is always available to be used during the student's unstructured time. And since the use of his unstructured time is at his own discretion, it can also be a hurdle in his program potential. In deciding whether he will be "in" or "out" of a particular resource center, the student is also learning to evaluate his interests, time, and responsibilities. The student who does not learn to direct his daily activities in such a manner as to take advantage of the resources available gains only from the structured part of the scheduled classes.

It is necessary to promote the idea of accessibility to instructional material centers during the school day. The students need to learn to use the time they have available to their best interests educationally, and this is not an easy task for all students. Certainly, it is not simply saying, "O.K., here are resource centers. Now, let's go ahead and use them." To make this assumption is an unfortunate mistake. Just as learning the correct use of the library should be a continual educational process in high school, certainly learning to use the resource centers has to be a growing program for all four years of the student's experience.

One of the advantages in increasing the library staff is the consultant service in the classroom that can be provided teachers. The associate librarian has the time to solicit opportunities from teachers to give book talks or to bring in a cart full of books and discuss them with a teacher and a small group of students. Informal discussions about the authors, making them a little more human, and some remarks regarding each book on the cart, personalizing the interest in reading and associating it with the current interests of the small group, is a helpful service which results in increased use of a variety of sources by students. When students participate in an informal discussion with the associate librarian and the teacher in this context, new and meaningful horizons are often revealed to them.

One of the interesting sidelights in using the associate librarian in this manner was the organization of a freshman library committee. This was a group of students interested in learning more about books and assisting the library in providing more varied and interesting services to freshmen. This group, functioning with the assistance of the associate librarian, was able to provide many worthwhile contributions of materials to the centers, as well as to the main library.

The orientation program for the freshman class starts immediately with the English and social studies teachers at the freshman level. This department of nine teachers has as one of its major concerns "bridging the gap" between the elementary and high school program. Introducing the basic concepts of the resource-center program and assisting students in working out independent-study patterns are part of the orientation unit.

The library orientation program is presented to freshman classes by the librarian during the first weeks of the school year.

This is a typical activity that takes place in many schools; however, because of the importance of proper use of the library and resource centers in the program at Marshall, it is further emphasized in all freshman classrooms as well as by the aides in resource centers. Students are encouraged to seek assistance from the resource-center aides and from the librarians. It is necessary at the very outset of the school year for all staff members to immediately assign work that will enable students to familiarize themselves with the available resources of the school. This approach to the teaching of library skills requires that we as teachers and staff have more and better instructional materials, and even more important that the teachers know what is available in resource centers and library for the teaching of a particular unit.

THE FRESHMAN ENGLISH AND SOCIAL STUDIES RESOURCE CENTER

The freshman English and social studies resource center was made from two standard classrooms with the contiguous nonbearing wall removed and one door blocked off so that the traffic necessarily passes by the aide's desk. In addition to the aforementioned list of aides' responsibilities, the freshman English–social studies aide has a special collection of over fifteen hundred general reading books primarily for freshmen who have reading difficulties. Assisting teachers in helping students to select and read from this special collection has been part of the freshman reading program since the resource center opened.

The aide in this center has had two years of college and is very interested in the English and social studies areas. She is a mother with children of her own in a high school. She sums up her responsibilities as follows:

> My main duty is to help the students. I do this by keeping their current supplementary materials readily available; by maintaining colorful, meaningful and occasionally amusing bulletin boards; by directing them to appropriate materials; and by maintaining an atmosphere conducive to study. I help the teachers in our department by making bibliographies; checking out special books to small groups of individuals; giving book talks to small groups to

> arouse interest in reading, particularly for the slow readers; and occasionally correcting papers or doing other work of this nature. The heavy attendance of students makes it impossible for me to do very much extra paper work, and our teachers are very understanding about this.

This is a very popular resource center and the usage increases year by year. Certainly one reason for this is the continual selection and purchase of more resource-center materials by teachers in the department. Knowing what is available in the center is a key to its successful operation. In this department each teacher spends two or more modules a week helping in the administration of the center, and in just helping students.

Students need time during the day to do their assignments, to do some independent thinking, to view materials related to assignments, to read more broadly, to conference with teachers, to discuss meaningful issues with fellow classmates, and to work on independent-study projects. We are trying to provide for most of these needs through the resource centers.

As our freshman English–social studies resource center is one of our most effective centers, it might be appropriate at this point to look briefly at what we would like to do to improve it. Certainly there is a continual need for more and greater varieties of instructional materials such as programmed materials, film loops, slides, and filmstrips. There is also, of course, a continual need for more supplementary materials for units that teachers are presenting. And of course it is essential that teachers continually develop knowledge of the resource-center materials in order that these materials can be used as an integral part of the units being taught. More individual-student study stations, or carrels, are needed. A look into the near future would indicate that these student stations will contain mechanical and electronic equipment connected to a central programmed computer; thus, in time computer-assisted instruction will be implemented for the student in the resource center during his independent-study time. And last, we are all agreed that wall-to-wall carpeting in the resource center would be a tremendous advantage, particularly in terms of atmosphere, student reaction, and acoustics.

A MULTIDEPARTMENTAL RESOURCE CENTER

The aide in the combined art, home economics, industrial arts, physical education and health resource center is a member of the teams in these departments. He works directly with the department chairmen in scheduling the activities of the center. Coordination is important, as the aide does a substantial amount of clerical work for teachers such as typing hand-out materials, tests, and other related materials.

The use of an aide by a department depends to a great extent on the talent of the aide. In this case because of a talent in the art area (a successful painter in oils with only a year to go for a teaching certificate), the aide has been called on occasionally for a large-group presentation, as a guest speaker, or for a small-group demonstration. Some other duties of this particular aide are to administer makeup tests, assist in the distribution of unit textbooks, maintain the center's collection and administer check-out procedures, assist in the development of slide sets for the slide projector and viewing area, coordinate teacher's use of audio-visual equipment, suggest possible books for purchase for the resource center based on the students' interests. This aide provides very effective and interesting displays and bulletin boards in order to make the center an attractive place for the student to work.

According to the aide and the four departments involved, the purpose of this center, as they see it, is to "Provide an area where students may study individually or together. To provide materials such as texts, reference books, magazines, slides, filmstrips, 8-mm film loops, and pamphlets for assignments, for independent-study projects, or for the personal interest of the student."

Students use the center to work on assignments that require the use of the above materials. Frequently the assignment is a "starting point" for independent study, or extra-credit projects. Students also use the center to peruse magazines related to the department, such as *House and Garden, Popular Mechanics, Sports Illustrated,* and many others. This is a well-organized center that illustrated how four departments can collaborate on the use of one aide for better utilization of required and supplementary instructional materials to provide for individual student needs.

THE LANGUAGE LABORATORY

The language lab, operated by a technician, is in a sense a resource center that plays an important part in our instructional-materials-center concept. The computer schedules students into the lab by language sections. At first level, students are scheduled for two separate twenty-minute modules per week. In addition, they are required to come to the lab two additional modules per week during unscheduled time. Roll is taken, and attendance is reflected in the grade. At advanced levels, the student is required to spend less time in the lab but is encouraged to use the lab as he feels the need. The language lab technician makes this center available to students for independent study every module of the day. Thus, this scheduling system allows the language lab to be utilized by both classes and individual students during the entire day.

Our present lab technician is a certified language teacher who is skilled in the use of the lab equipment. This consists of a seven-channel console with tape decks and record player. Around the perimeter of the room are listening stations where students may listen to tapes independently during their unscheduled time. These units are all controlled through the console.

The lab technician is available to the students for aid in their language study. Also, she helps the student get the most out of the listening experience by working very closely with the language teachers. In some cases the language teacher handles the lab and uses the technician to assist.

The language technician prepares tapes for teachers, corrects papers, and assists in bulletin-board preparation. The technician works closely with the language teachers to present a well-rounded course of language study.

THE GRAPHIC ARTIST—A NECESSITY

The graphic artist is a very important person in our instructional materials department. He provides the teacher with a readily available resource and consultant service and is in effect an instructional resource for teachers. The transparencies, slides, charts, and other materials he produces are very important to the success of large-group presentations. Many ideas that are lost because of a lack of teacher time for the implementation in the traditional program are conferenced with the teacher and the graphic artist and then placed on the drawing board for visual presentation.

The securing of a graphic artist was one of the top priorities as we moved into the new program. The position requires an imaginative and creative person, experienced in layout, drawing, color, and the use of equipment that will facilitate the visual production work of the department. This person should be one who is professionally trained in drawing, sketching, and cartooning—an "idea man"—and one who likes to work with teachers and students. The graphic artist must be able to develop an intuitive grasp of the teacher's ideas and then be able to convey these ideas to the students with exciting and appropriate visual aids. The graphic artist works directly with the teachers and librarian in organizing this part of the instructional-materials-center program.

By providing this important service to teachers and staff, this graphic artist enriches all presentations in all curricula. The following is a brief outline of services performed thus far by our graphic artist:

1. Conceiving, designing, drawing projection visuals for use in large groups and for use in the resource centers
   a. Overhead transparencies
   b. Slides—35-mm
   c. Film loops—8-mm
   d. Filmstrips
2. Using photography to develop illustrations for a variety of display purposes
3. Helping teachers, aides, and students with their bulletin-board displays
   a. Ideas and design
   b. Artwork
   c. Lettering

4. Producing signs—instructive, decorative, informative—for general school use
5. Producing publications and a variety of printed matter
   a. Layout
   b. Artwork
   c. Photography
   d. Lettering

The graphic artist works closely with the teaching staff in experimenting with new ideas. Teachers now have professional assistance in developing visual materials primarily for large-group presentations and for individual student use. It is inconceivable to us to successfully implement a modular-flexible program with all its innovative components without the services of a full-time competent graphic artist.

THE COMMUNICATIONS LABORATORY

The communications lab is a recent but most important part of the instructional-materials-center concept at Marshall High School. The primary objective of the reading consultant and the two aides working in the lab is to improve the competence of students in reading, writing, listening, and speaking. The lab was established under the direction of an excellent reading consultant in the fall of 1966 as part of a Title I, ESEA project. Students were selected on the basis of reading needs. Referred by teachers, the reading consultant conferenced with the student and then scheduled him into the program if the student wanted this kind of assistance. No pressure is put on the student to enroll, but rather, he is made to feel that it is a privilege to become a participant in the communications lab program. Counselors and teachers may refer students to the lab. The student comes in for an interview, and for testing if necessary, and upon selection is given an orientation on how to use the lab to his advantage.

Some English classes are scheduled into this class for special instruction. Sometimes the materials and some equipment are transported to the classroom for a specially prepared lesson by the reading consultant.

Another service of the lab is that of providing teachers reading materials, ideas, and techniques in the teaching of reading skills. Teachers are familiar with the consultant service available, and all have some background on reading problems. The majority of the staff have attended reading workshops conducted by the reading consultant and designed for the needs of their departments. These workshops were the result of a teacher reading committee, which spearheads the reading improvement program for the school. This committee, representing teachers in a number of areas of the curriculum—health, home economics, English, biology, counseling, industrial arts, and social studies—has taken the responsibility of piloting some of the reading concepts in their classes. The statement of philosophy of the reading committee is as follows:

> A definite relationship exists between success in reading and success in school, in daily living, and in the world of work. Because students are individuals, not statistics, they must be accepted at their own levels of performance, effective, developmental or remedial, and have realistic reading programs planned on that basis. This can be accomplished only through the efforts of teachers in all areas of the curriculum. The Marshall reading committee believes:
>
> 1. All students can and need to improve their reading competencies.
> 2. All teachers can and should help students to develop their potentialities in these competencies.
> 3. The basic reading skills can and should be applied in any area or subject where words are used for thinking, listening, talking, reading, or writing.
> 4. The reading committee should help implement in-service programs which will provide teachers with the latest techniques for teaching reading.

A half-unit course in communications skills for all freshmen with general reading problems was an outgrowth of the communications lab. This course was a result of the team efforts of the reading consultant and the speech department. The speaking and listening skills of the freshmen are one of the primary concerns of our speech department and the communications lab. A teaching aide working with the reading consultant developed a program in oral communications that was most satisfactory. The goals and objectives for this program were consistent with those of the entire Portland program for slow learners, specifically:

A. To improve listening:
1. Following instructions
2. Taking notes
3. Reacting to impressions
4. Relating ideas

B. To improve speaking:
1. Improving pronunciation
2. Adopting acceptable usage
3. Practicing courtesy in discussion
4. Gaining easy confidence in speaking
5. Enjoying the process of oral communication

"CLUB FORTY-FIVE"—A SPECIAL CENTER

Some students shy away from resource centers or the library. These are usually students who do not enjoy reading and who do not read as well as they should. With this problem in mind, our English department developed an action program that would involve the slow learners, primarily of the "45 Club," to motivate them toward reading enjoyment. The result, it was hoped, was to make a more proficient reader of the student. To accomplish this goal, the English department rescheduled classroom B–45 so that only teachers in the English C program used the room. The entire project was under the direction of the English department chairman and an English teacher who served as general chairman of the "45 Club." Under the general chairman's leadership, the following steps were taken to develop this center:

1. Worked with teachers and students on four grade levels to organize program
2. Checked room utilization sheets
3. Rescheduled classes
4. Verified room transfers
5. Recruited volunteers for selecting materials and displays
6. Arranged for book deliveries
7. Secured suitable magazine and book racks
8. Coordinated the efforts of teachers from *several* departments to ensure adequate supervision
9. Oriented teachers and students alike concerning club policies
10. Arranged for student assistants during and after each school day
11. Arranged for several hundred student passes

The result was a transformation of a standard-size classroom (30 by 30 feet) into a lounge-type reading center with student appeal.

The "selling" feature of the room, however, appears to be the luxurious wall-to-wall carpeting, not available in any other room in the school, on which students stretch out to read. Bright throw pillows added a touch of informality to the room.

Interest in "Club 45" spread throughout the student body. To accommodate other interested students throughout the day, volunteer student assistants aid in supervising the room. All students scheduled in the English C program, as well as all assistants, must carry the official membership card. This card lends the club atmosphere to the room, even though any interested student may be issued a card. Students in the C program are scheduled into the room one class period a week. Any member, C student or assistant, may enter the room at any time. Many students are spending much of their unstructured time every week browsing or reading the Club materials. The "45 Club" appears to be an exciting innovation in the learning process of the student. This center has provided many teachers with a new tool to work with students on reading. "Read!, Read!, Read!" is the motto of this center.

THE LIBRARY—HEART OF THE RESOURCE-CENTER COMPLEX

The development of the instructional-materials-center concept necessarily required a new working relationship between the vice-principal for curriculum and instruction and the librarian. In accepting the new philosophy of materials centers, the librarian quite automatically became more directly involved with the curriculum of the high school. The extension of library services into resource centers, the new media available to the librarian, and the possibility of more assistance in research for the classroom teachers—all these ideas afforded a clarification of the new roles of the librarian and the associate librarian. The headquarters staff for the main library, which is the heart of the instructional materials center, consists of the librarian, associate librarian, two library clerks, a textbook clerk, an audio-visual clerk, and a graphic artist.

The duties and responsibilities of the librarian, the director of the instructional materials center at John Marshall High School, are listed below:

I. Primary responsibilities: materials consultant and coordinator of library and resource centers
  A. Selection-acquisition: storage, retrieval, circulation of materials
  B. Range of materials: textbooks, supplementary texts, books, pamphlets, periodicals, audio-visual hardware and materials
  C. For: library and resource centers

II. Areas of responsibilities
  A. Main library
    1. Hours of primary responsibility: 7:30 to 11:30 A.M.
    2. Duties: supervision, reference, desk-type work
  B. Resource centers
    1. Basic responsibility for all centers
    2. Specifically: English, English–social studies, and social studies
    3. Peripheral areas: language lab, reading lab, B–45
      a. Selection of materials in conjunction with department chairmen, teachers, and teacher aides

    b. Help with organization and circulation of materials
    c. Planning with departments and teams
  C. Audio-visual materials
  D. Textbooks and supplementary texts

III. Personnel to supervise
  A. Associate librarian
  B. Library clerks
  C. Book-room clerk
  D. Audio-visual clerk
  E. Graphic artist
  F. Resource-center aides
  G. Departmental clerks
  H. Student assistants in the library

IV. Obligations to faculty and students
  A. Department chairman–curriculum associate committee
  B. Read current periodicals to bridge gap in Readers' Guide indexing
  C. Circulate review books to faculty members, aides, and students for their opinions and comments
  D. Review books for monthly librarians' meetings
  E. Compile broad-scope subject bibliographies for teachers and departments
  F. Introduce incoming freshmen to using the library through English–social studies classes
  G. Assist teachers in presenting the use of the library to their students
  H. Give book talks to classes
  I. Make classroom presentations on how to approach research work, how to use indexes and Readers' Guide, resources available at the public library, etc.

The associate librarian was selected to work primarily with the departments in setting up the resource centers and working with the aides in the centers as they developed policy and increased their collections. She now works directly with only one-half of the resource centers and is thus able to spend much more of her time in the main library. The following are duties and responsibilities of the associate librarian:

I. Supervision of the business education, art–home economics–industrial arts, mathematics–science, and foreign language resource centers
   - *A.* Select, order and prepare materials (i.e., shelf listing and cataloging of all materials in resource centers to date)
   - *B.* Analyze resource center aides' jobs in order to understand personnel problems, instruct substitutes, etc.

II. Coordination of radio and TV programming, educational and commercial
   - *A.* Oversee the use of the TV set and earphones
   - *B.* Post announcements on bulletin board in lounge, library, and front office (also in ESS teachers' offices)
   - *C.* Inform individual teachers of specific programs

III. Assistance in supervision of library
   - *A.* Do floor work in afternoons
     1. Assist students in selection and location of books
     2. Assist students in reference questions
   - *B.* Operate and maintain Xerox machine
   - *C.* Collect library fines
   - *D.* Assist in cataloging
   - *E.* Have an understanding of the clerical functions of the library
   - *F.* Oversee the mending and repair of books
   - *G.* Prepare display case in main hall

IV. Obligation to faculty and students
   - *A.* Review books—monthly review meeting
   - *B.* Circulate review books to faculty members and aides for their opinions and comments
   - *C.* Compile bibliographies
   - *D.* Give assistance to those teachers who teach the use of the library and its tools
   - *E.* Serve on the reading committee

The new role of the librarians in a school is easy to define but sometimes rather difficult to implement if the proper atmosphere is not created. The librarians, the administrators, the department chairmen, and the teaching staff must work together as a team to develop library and resource centers as functional places for learning within the total concept of the instructional materials center.

7

English Course Structures: Approaches to More Effective Teaching

James R. Barchek

No one is more aware of the need for improvement in the teaching of English than English teachers themselves. For years they have complained about the many areas of inefficiency and conflict that exist between what should be going on in English classrooms and one-hour-a-day, five-day-a-week English classes with thirty-five students in them that exist in most schools. For years English teachers have known that learning experiences were often hindered by traditional teacher loads and methods of organization. Many different activities are carried on in English classes, but some common classroom objectives are almost assuredly shared by all. Improvement of student writing is probably the most common goal and is usually approached in two ways: instruction in fundamentals or technique; and drill or actual writing, which is evaluated in the hope that the evaluation will beget improvement. Yet in a traditional program, a number of weaknesses are apparent. Instruction, whether it be a lecture or demonstration or a film or record or any means of simply presenting material to students, must be repeated over and over again and perhaps duplicated by other teachers down the hall who have similar classes. Even writing themes or doing drills in class is expensive in terms of teacher time, a valuable commodity. But perhaps the most important facet of composition teaching is the refinement of an individual student's writing. One of the great difficulties in teaching composition in high school is that no two students are writing at exactly the same level of proficiency. And since what we desire in writing is the steady growth of an extremely complex process which has been taught to classes and practiced by each individual student since the primary grades in varying degrees of sophistication, individual instruction is a necessity. Good teachers have been trying for years to fit individual conference time into a schedule designed to take care of groups, knowing all the time that nothing is as meaningful and effective in improving writing as conferences with one student, one teacher, and one paper.

Teaching literature also involves some basic methods: presenting background and motivational material necessary for teaching a particular work; and some study in depth in which students can proceed through a process of criticism or analysis, testing ideas and reacting to others' ideas about the work being studied. Yet in literature again, we must repeat and duplicate in presentation of material and struggle through discussion periods with a group so large that even if every student did desire to participate, there would not be enough time in a class period to allow it. Recent curriculum studies in English almost unanimously endorse an increased emphasis on inductive teaching, on direct involvement of the student with the material he is studying; yet the existence of large numbers of students in today's large high schools dictates large classes—poor conditions for the inductive process to take place.

It was with all this in mind that the staff of Marshall High School decided to make a real change in the nature of the school's organization. Although Marshall was a traditionally designed and organized high school before the fall of 1963, it was a relatively new school with few traditions about courses or personnel. Its administrators and its faculty were young, liberal, willing to accept and even initiate change. From the very beginning, there was an air of experimentation in the school: Teachers were gingerly trying "team teaching" by exchanging classes one day a week or for one unit to allow a teacher with a special interest in some specific area like modern poetry or linguistics to teach his interest to more than one class. One English teacher who had prepared a series of lessons on the history of the language traveled around to different senior English classes presenting this unit, a total of eleven different times in one year. No doubt, this was an improvement over the completely isolated English classroom in which only his students would have received much instruction in this area, but it was a cumbersome and inefficient method at best. He was forced to leave his classroom too often, and the teachers whose classes he instructed had to teach his students. Consequently they missed the lessons of the language history unit in their classrooms and were unable to answer questions that might come up the next day or help with assignments or discuss a language history lesson with their students. The next year an attempt at greater efficiency was tried. Since the building contained some large classrooms with folding doors, the unit on language history was presented in one block five times each day; and all senior English teachers who wished their classes to attend brought them to the large room. This was an improvement over the previous year: The number of presentations was cut in half and teachers were able to attend the sessions with their classes (those teachers who brought more than one class even gained a period to correct papers or plan lessons after they had observed the lesson once). Still the greater efficiency only made it more apparent that there was room for much more improvement. This particular example is typical of the experiments that were going on throughout the department. Teachers were breaking up classes into smaller groups, using student teachers and student chairmen to supervise and to lead discussions; able students—even some small classes—were being dismissed one or two days a week for "independent study." Special rooms were set aside for study centers for selected students. Although only a relatively small part of the department was directly engaged in experiments of this type, the entire department was aware that they were going on; and all teachers were interested in their successes and failures. Consequently, when the opportunity came to engage the entire school in a new program, the department was ready to make a decision based on an already instilled interest and a knowledgeable background.

PLANNING AND IMPLEMENTING NEW TEACHING AND LEARNING STRATEGIES

The original decision itself was made by the entire faculty but was not considered binding on all individual faculty members. English teams were created by individual faculty members who wanted to join together to teach. Each teacher had the option of working by himself in a traditional classroom. But the excitement seemed contagious: Before long every English teacher had decided to at least try a new approach for a year.

The program under consideration by the English department was influenced by a number of sources. English teachers, like the others, were aware of some of the writings of J. Lloyd Trump. Because of their college training and the Portland Curriculum Study with its resultant institutes, most had been influenced by the "New Critic" approach to literature and its corresponding increased use of an inductive, analytical approach to teaching. But the real source of authority came from experience and past attempts at experimentation with its corresponding evaluation and modification. With very little literature on the subject in general and almost no practical research in the area of class length and size specifically relating to English, teachers drew heavily on their past successes and failures in an attempt to create a new, more effective means of organizing the English faculty, the English classroom, the entire instructional process in English.

The key was *learning*. Teams started organizing their courses by considering a number of questions based on the learning process of their subject matter: What exactly should students learn in this particular course? What particular learning experiences occur in individual lessons? How much time does it take to learn this? In what size group can this learning take place most effectively? How many times per week should certain learning activities take place? In what sequence should learning activities be organized? How can students learn outside class? Each team in this way created its own course structure. There is no standard English department course structure: A prime advantage of the flexible schedule is that each course structure is designed around its unique body of knowledge and its own students by those who best know that body of knowledge and those students.

Although the English teams decided upon differing course structures for different courses, it was to be expected that there would be a great deal of similarity: English courses share a number of practices and objectives. We know that for some learning activities, class size is not important, that students can listen and observe as effectively in a large group as a small one. Consequently all English courses included in their course structure a large group which met for thirty-six minutes once each week. The first year some teachers, dubious about very large groups, split courses with 150 total enrollment into two large-group sections of 75 each. After one year there was unanimous agreement that once class size exceeds 35, there is no advantage to limiting it any further, that neither discipline nor an attention factor was related to number. Since then, all large groups have met with all the students enrolled in that particular course meeting in one section. English large groups, then, run from 60 to 400 students. Films, records, panels, lectures, dramatizations, and guest speakers (who are much more willing to come to schools when guaranteed an audience of this size) are used. The most significant advantage gained in large-group teaching is efficiency. Teacher time is conserved so that it may be more effectively used in other learning activities which are costly in terms of teacher time but effective in terms of learning. But the large group is an important phase of the total program. The combination of large numbers of students and other teachers in the audience coupled with the fact that some planning time has been provided has resulted in teachers preparing consistently superior presentations. The staff assumed at the beginning that some teachers would discover a talent for large-group work and others would perhaps tend to specialize in small group, but this failed to develop. Instead, teachers have tended to emphasize some subject-matter specialty such as linguistics or composition or Shakespeare or modern poetry. Each member of the team makes the large-group presentations in the area of his specialty. This specialization by content rather than specialization by teaching mode has been well accepted at Marshall after several years of experience.

Once each week students also attend a writing lab varying in size from 30 to 70. In these large double rooms stocked with large numbers of dictionaries and writing handbooks and equipped with an elevated teaching platform, an overhead projector, and a microphone, students are taught and practice composition, take tests, give speeches, and drill. Some large labs are staffed with two teachers working as a team. It is thereby possible to gain the flexibility of working with a group of 70 for economical presentation of material, which frees one member of the team for lesson planning and paper correction, or of breaking the group into two classes of 35 when the activity seems better suited to a smaller group. Labs vary in length from sixty to eighty minutes.

It was originally decided that some activities worked very well in groups of 30 to 35 students; consequently most courses included a medium group in their structure once a week. After a couple of years, however, teachers seemed to feel that this group tended to become a place where material was presented to students (less efficiently than in large group), or where students took tests or wrote (at greater expense of teacher time in a lab), or where a discussion took place (much less effectively than in small group). The medium group has consequently disappeared from English course structures.

Whenever teacher time was available, the medium group was replaced with a second small-group meeting to bring the number of class meetings to four per week. Each student meets at least once each week in a small seminar group of 8 to 16 for close analytic discussion of literature, language, or composition. The thought of finally having small discussion groups was one of the most exciting prospects of the modular schedule for English teachers, something they had been seeking for years. However, the small group turned out to be one of the most difficult phases for teachers to master. With little experience and no training, teachers found that lively, stimulating exchanges of ideas did not come automatically with a reduction in class size. It took almost a year of careful attention, experimentation, and discussion of method before teachers felt that small groups were consistently effective. Although the staff knew that the major role of the small group is for student interaction, it was difficult for some teachers to keep from dominating the discussion. Through continual study, experimentation, and assessment of small-group techniques, most teachers now agree that the original purpose of the small group is valid; and they conscientiously attempt to maintain effective and worthwhile student discussion. If a close, analytic look at a poem or essay or issue is needed, the small group is used for this, sometimes student led, sometimes teacher led. If something especially complicated or difficult needs to be presented, something which would best be done with students interacting closely with the material being presented, the small group is the mode generally used. The important thing is that the learning experience be determined first—in terms of the total learning pattern—and that the most efficient teaching-learning mode be selected in which that learning experience can take place.

All courses in English use large-group and small-group phases in their structures, but there are a number of modifications in the basic pattern of meetings. Small seminar courses for especially able and interested students meet almost exclusively in small group, with the option of attending the large group at the discretion of the teacher or student. Their total time in class per week is less than that of the average student. The courses for students weak in language skills, on the other hand, total more time per week in class than the average, much of it in lab phases where they may work under direct supervision. Teachers of nonacademic classes also found it advantageous to specify "exclusive student sectioning" in order to maintain group integrity when building their course structures, ensuring that student groups stayed together through their various phases and that the same teacher met with them for all phases. Teachers of upper-level advanced courses, however, do not feel that it is important to maintain this personal contact; they feel that any group could meet with any member of the team and that what is more important is the order in which phases occur. Teachers of special English elective courses like drama, speech, journalism, and effective reading created totally different structures based on what is best suited in terms of class size and length to their own unique activities. However, English teachers have not been able to implement an ideal program—the "perfect" English course structure is simply too expensive. Small groups are costly in terms of teacher time. A course with an enrollment of 150 in small groups of 13 students meeting for forty minutes once each week, for example, takes eight hours of teacher time. Teachers would prefer students to meet two or three times per week in small group, but the addition of one small-group meeting for eleven sections increases the teacher workload by eight hours per week. The addition of a lab of 75 students for the same time costs the team only eighty minutes. English teachers would often like to determine the sequence of phases, specifying, for example, that large group must be followed by small group 1, lab, medium group, and small group 2, in that order. But it was found that specifications this complex were simply too restrictive in terms of students' programs. English teachers, consequently, have never believed that they have the ultimate English course structure. It is generally agreed, however, that in spite of these limitations a substantial improvement in facilitating learning has been made. What is most important is that teachers built the course structure around their students and their subject matter and created, as far as limitations of staff time and schoolwide programs made possible, a structure designed to facilitate the learning process in their particular course.

But there is more to a student's total English experience than the classwork. Independent study has become an integral part of the English courses. Independent study was perhaps the most difficult phase of the program to implement on an effective basis. Like small group, it was not a part of teachers' training or experience, and it was a completely foreign concept to students. English teachers realized, however, that without an effective independent-study program, the full potential of the program would not be realized. A group of English teachers organized a committee to implement a working independent-study phase within and around the English curriculum. Since that initial effort, the committee and the concept of independent study has become schoolwide and has grown to include students with a wide range of interests and abilities. Successful English projects range from a freshman's attempts to find answers to questions that came up in small group like, "Why were sports so important to the Greeks?" to a senior's involved study of stage design, a project which culminated in the design of a stage and setting for a modern play. English, and English teachers, often play a large part in a student's independent-study project in some other area, such as science. Problems of organization, bibliography, the reporting of almost any project can involve English teachers.

The English resource center, a departmental library built in a large room in the department wing, is stocked with over two thousand volumes relevant to the study of English, ranging from magazines and easy-to-read paperback novels to critical works on Chaucer and a set of *The Oxford English Dictionary.* It is not intended to replace the school library. The works contained in it are specifically related to the study of English, mostly reference works and collections with a few novels relating to the work of a particular course. The English resource center seats eighty and is staffed with a teacher aide who knows the curriculum, the students, and the available materials. Students are encouraged to come in and work or browse during their unscheduled time.

One of the most important phases of the English program at Marshall is the individual conference time provided both teachers and students. Each English teacher posts office hours on the conference rooms connected to the resource center indicating the times he is available for student conferences. These conferences have proved to be an important phase of many teachers' composition program, and they are an extremely important phase of independent study. One of the most disappointing aspects of English teaching is the knowledge that after all those hours spent correcting papers, many students do not understand the little red marks or do not bother to read the critical comments on their papers. Their revisions of later papers show exactly the same errors over and over again. A conference can never assure that students will be unsatisfied with less than their best on their next paper (one of the biggest problems in trying to improve a skill), but it can assure the teacher that a student knows where he used a run-on sentence or where his thesis lacks support or is too general. The teacher can ask questions rather than point out errors, leading the student to discover some of his own faults; or the teacher can ask him to modify or correct errors orally until he is sure the student understands. Together they can, even should, agree on an individual goal for improvement, agreeing, for example, that one student will concentrate on trying more mature sentence patterns in the next theme and another will pay especial attention to organization or supporting details. In this way teacher and student can work out a highly individualized writing program within the scope of the regular curriculum and the normal writing assignments for the course. This is only possible, however, when both student and teacher have time to meet in this manner. If a teacher spends five hours a week in this way and spends fifteen minutes on the average with each student, he can see over eighty students a month. The average teacher, then, will see his students less than once a month. Those willing to spend more time will see students more frequently, but even once every six weeks is enough to put some humanity into writing courses, many of which are too mechanical and impersonal to accomplish much with what is essentially a highly personal art.

Goals that include attitudes, values, and individual development are difficult to measure; however, it is apparent that a number of encouraging things are happening. Students respond well to the responsibility placed upon them. They find their own materials and use them. They read and react as individuals more than under the former traditional design. The study of English has increasingly become a personal interaction with the discipline, instead of a kind of mass bus tour through Concord and Stratford.

Teachers are busy in this program, perhaps busier than they have ever been; but they are busy doing things only an English teacher can do. The teacher aide in the resource center and the English department clerk are able to relieve them of many jobs that are important but may not necessarily require someone with a degree in English and years of teaching experience to perform. Classroom time is cut down to free teachers for planning, individual conferences, or other duties, so that the time that is left is used as efficiently as possible. For example, teachers no longer waste a period picking up and checking in books and checking out new ones—and then running down lost copies and forgetful students and filling out slips and more slips. When a unit is finished, a teacher simply announces in large group, "Turn in your copies of *Julius Caesar*, and bring *The Scarlet Letter* to your next small group." Students then go to the English resource center during their unscheduled time, turn in their old books, and receive new ones; the entire process is taken care of by a student helper supervised by the teacher aide. Countless jobs like this—typing, duplicating, record keeping, correcting objective tests—that once took the time of an English teacher are now done very efficiently by paraprofessionals and students under their supervision. When it was decided that the English department would be allotted a teacher aide and a clerk, teachers discussed possible uses of their time. It was suggested that paper readers be hired to relieve teachers of part of the time spent in reading themes. The English teachers decided, however, that reading themes was something a trained, experienced teacher who worked with students *should* do and that if they could be relieved of some of the clerical work which every teacher spends much time doing, they would read their own themes. Experience seems to have borne out the wisdom of this decision: The close contacts brought about through the small-group, independent-study, and individual-conference phases of the English program are facilitated to a large extent by teachers who work closely with individual students. Reading a student's papers—carefully—is a necessary part of this contact. English teachers work together sharing ideas and talents and problems and generally cooperating much more than most English teachers in a traditional school, and not only because of team teaching: They do so because the entire process of teaching English to the students of Marshall High School has come out into the open to be observed, discussed, evaluated, revised, and strengthened by all the people involved.

AN ENGLISH TEACHER'S DAY IN THE NEW DESIGN

The result of this complete overhaul of the school and department machinery is a change in the very nature of an English teacher's job. His day begins, now, at the English department office. English teachers no longer have their own room; the departmental office serves as a home base. The office, created out of a large storage room, was carpeted and painted, equipped with desks and file cabinets for each teacher and with tables and chairs for team planning and reading. The department clerk works here, and typewriters and a ditto machine are provided for teachers to use. The office is designed to facilitate a cooperative approach to planning and teaching and to provide an area for teachers to work as individuals and as teams. After dropping his coat and materials at his desk, the English teacher probably starts with a short registration period in some classroom and then begins his teaching day.

He may begin with a small group of advanced students (his schedule includes more small groups than any other kind of class each week). He meets his small group, about thirteen students, in a classroom in the English wing and begins the discussion. For thirty-six minutes, he tries to maintain a rather precarious balance between keeping the discussion focused on the subject the team planned without dominating the thinking of the group, answering questions of fact that may facilitate the discussion, raising questions that may stimulate the thinking, prodding individuals to keep them involved and to keep some members from completely dominating the group, and fighting the impulse to point out fallacies immediately and provide the answers which seem so obvious but which he knows students should arrive at by themselves.

After the small group, he picks up a cup of coffee, goes back to the English office for his weekly one-hour B-team planning session. (He belongs to two teams: one for the advanced course and one for the regular course, both on the same grade level.) For the next hour, he talks with members of his team about the successes and problems of the current unit and the goals of the next unit, discussing—even arguing perhaps—about the best approach until an agreement among team members is reached concerning what basic goals and approaches will be taken; what materials will be covered in the large group; what should focus the small-group discussions; what should be done in writing lab; what films, records, or other teaching aids should be used; and who will be responsible for the various phases.

Following team planning session, he goes to a large writing lab which he teaches with one of the other members of his team. Today his teammate is giving a twenty-minute presentation on the use of concrete details in writing. While this is going on, he works in the next room with five or six students who need help with sentence structure. After twenty minutes, these students join the main group for the assignment and writing of a theme. Once the students begin writing, his teammate, who made the presentation, leaves to correct the papers of the previous lab. He stays and circulates around the room while the students write, helping those who need help, raising questions for some, complimenting others, suggesting conferences or references or further readings to those who need or seem interested in them.

After lunch and another small group, he spends an hour in the English resource center in individual conference with students. A girl wants to do an independent-study project on different translations of the Bible but complains, "There just isn't any material in town." Three of his lab students bring in revisions of themes to be discussed, and one boy comes in just to talk about a novel he has just finished. It would have been easy to stay another hour, but large group begins in a few minutes, and so he leaves the resource center and goes to the small auditorium to make certain the equipment he plans to use is working and adjusted. A short bell rings, and he stands there at the front of the auditorium watching while two hundred students pour in, filling the front half of the room. After a quick glance to assure that his teammates have started taking roll, he begins: "Shakespeare's language *does* look strange to us. Today I'm going to talk about some of the reasons for its strangeness." For the next thirty minutes, he talks to 200 advanced juniors about the nature of the English language in the early seventeenth century, using the overhead projector to show examples of Elizabethan prose and a page from the first folio; talking about differences in the alphabet and in spelling practices; playing a short selection from a record of someone reading a passage from a Shakespearean play and another excerpt of someone reading the same passage, pronouncing the words as they were probably pronounced at the time the play was written. His eyes move over the large group constantly, looking for signs of failure to understand or lack of interest, going back over his material or changing the pace if needed. With an eye on the clock, he finishes, ". . . but there is another, perhaps more important, reason Shakespeare's characters don't talk in what seems to us to be normal conversational English—even for the early seventeenth century. Be sure to bring your books to small group where we will be taking a close look at the way Shakespeare uses poetry in a play." The bell rings, the chatter begins, and 200 students pour out of the exits while he clicks off the equipment; gathers up his notes, records, and projectuals; and answers questions for the couple of students who want to talk or argue about a point raised in the lecture.

"The last three modules and no more classes scheduled," he thinks. "A good time to get some work done." Picking his way out of the auditorium through the three hundred students now filing in for the social studies large group following his, he walks down the hall to the teachers' lounge. A couple of men teachers are in the corner arguing with the coach about last week's game, but the thought of seventy lab papers to correct makes him decide to do as he planned—get a cup of coffee and take it down to the English department office and start correcting them. Halfway across the office to his desk he hears his name called by one of the members of a sophomore team. Picking up his coffee cup, he casts one last glance at his stack of uncorrected papers and walks over to their team planning session. "What do you think of using *Lord of the Flies* for our advanced sophomores?" he is asked.

The sound of students passing by on their way home for the day is the first indication that they have been talking excitedly for an hour. It is 3:15 and not one paper has been corrected. "Team leaders' meeting until 4:30," he thinks. "Oh well, I'll take the papers home—again."

8

Science Course Structures: Some New Approaches to Learning

William H. Oberteuffer

The school year of 1962–1963 was a great year of opportunity for the science staff at John Marshall High School. Many of us had become increasingly aware that our school was not doing the sort of job it should. It was a very adequate school, perhaps a good one. But schools in general were not (and are not yet) fully accepting the challenge of the fast-changing world. Educators recognize that most young children are curious and love to learn but that too often by middle elementary grades some of them already dislike school. And schools had changed very little in response. Yet we had often seen business and industry adopt new methods as rapidly as new needs became apparent.

ASSESSING THE TRADITIONAL

Then that fall in 1962 the faculty stopped to ponder, "How can we at Marshall better keep pace with the new society?" The school itself was in its third year of operation, and the faculty had not fallen into a rigid pattern. Marshall High School's administration was young, vigorous, and eager to try new ideas that might enable education to serve the real needs of all the students. Ideas from many sources began to ferment. Strong leadership plus good fellowship within the Marshall staff resulted in the birth of a new program.

For the science department this meant time, space, and freedom to experiment with the new nationally developed courses in chemistry, physics, and biology that we were teaching in order to more fully utilize their unique features as well as to find new ways to squeeze every advantage from the subject matter and the class and lab experiences.

Science, perhaps more than any other subject, was beginning to feel the effect of the knowledge explosion. Depending upon which scientist you listened to, knowledge was doubling every seven or ten years. Neither scientist nor science teacher could keep up with this increasing volume of knowledge. Should we expect students to learn at this new rate? We realized that we must be willing to revamp the contents of the courses, perhaps to restructure the entire approach.

Science teachers had taught certain things in their courses for a long time. Those of us who were experienced had a much greater problem in this respect than the newcomers to the profession. We had taught frog dissection, gasoline motors, or water decomposition so long we thought these units had to be in our courses. We did not expect to be asked, "Why?"; and if asked, we could not always give satisfactory reasons. Why should a student learn to label the numbered parts of a crayfish, for instance? Would it diminish his appreciation of life or lessen his ability to cope with it if he did not know the parts of the grasshopper? We had begun to understand why students questioned aspects of the sacred curriculum. And had not many teachers been discouraged by trying to teach all the traditional course of study as well as the supplemental units added to keep the course up to date?

Method as well as content was being questioned. Certainly in science, a teacher could not know everything. A science teacher does not go to class long before he either shams or says, "I don't know." With the present knowledge explosion, we could no longer fit the pattern that had been established for teachers in this country over the past several hundred years—a pattern that pictured a teacher as a person who knows all the answers.

Some of us had become convinced that teaching is not telling. We thought that instead of just lecturing and testing students on facts, we should be asking students questions, stimulating discussion, encouraging wide reading, letting them explore and discover principles in the laboratory. We had begun to see the teacher as one who directs a wide variety of activities designed to help all students understand the principles of science and be prepared to apply them.

Learning is an entirely personal thing. It takes place inside a student. People need time to learn. They must be given time to become involved in what they are doing. They must be given time to experience and to think; and they certainly must know why they are in class.

We had seen increasing evidence that poor relationships in the classroom between students and between students and teachers had a limiting effect upon their interest in learning or upon their ability to learn. It seemed that most students must develop some kind of "we" or group feeling before education is truly efficient. Imagine students who had come to class all year long and did not even know the names of the other people in the class. How could they feel as if they were student-teacher team members and were working on a common goal in the spirit of sharing and acceptance prerequisite to wholehearted participation? It seemed there was a great deal we could and must do to promote a feeling of personal commitment, self-confidence, and safeness on the part of individual students, so that they could develop the freedom to express themselves.

The science department at Marshall High School has good laboratory facilities and was already teaching primarily laboratory-oriented courses, such as the PSSC physics, Chem Study chemistry, Yellow Version BSCS biology, and "Designs of the Cosmos," a physical science course originated in the Portland public schools. We had felt, as science teachers generally have felt, the need for more laboratory time. We had sensed, without doing much about it, the need for variability in the program to accommodate the wide ranges of needs, interests, and abilities of the students in our classes.

In our science courses, we were not looking primarily for students who might go into science, although occasionally we would find a promising young scientist. We were most interested in educating a science-literate society, badly needed at the present time in this country. We felt there was a real danger that before long, if not now, a majority of voters would be paying for or rejecting civic or national enterprises which they did not understand. The continued existence of a scientific aristocracy did not bode well for the future of this country as a democracy. In order to develop science-literate citizens, we must try to help students learn science by "sciencing." For instance, there is not one scientific method. There are scientific methods innumerable, and any one of them that works for a given purpose is the one you want to use for that job.

We were concerned that we teach "thinking," but most groups of teenagers could not be expected to sit down and study "thinking" as such. They needed to have something to think about, and we think about science in our classes. Because science requires both, we emphasize creative and critical thinking. This places heavy demands on each teacher to do the same in order to serve as a model and to create a classroom climate that stimulates, necessitates, and rewards creative and critical thinking and the behavior that they imply. Unless we practice what we teach, we cannot expect that our students will. Dr. William Burton in his book, *Education for Effective Thinking*[1], relates a man's style of thinking to his behavior: "Without a disposition to act critically, there is little likelihood that a person will consistently respond to situations in a manner which can properly be described as critical thinking."

Unless both teachers and students are free to test hypotheses, to follow logical conclusions, and to apply the new models that accrue from this increased critical and creative thought—even when this includes the unexpected, uncomfortable, or unusual—then training, not education, is taking place, and the same power and privilege games that are now substituted for education will continue to thwart involvement in learning. For instance, lab work of the past has involved primarily verifying facts that had already

[1] William Burton, Roland Kimball, and Richard Wing, *Education for Effective Thinking*, Appleton-Century-Crofts, Inc., New York, 1960. pp. 426–427.

been presented to the student in lectures or textbooks, filling in lab books and taking part in semi- or nonmeaningful large-group laboratory exercises. The new science programs involve real experiences in the laboratory, results of which can not be readily anticipated.

PLANNING AND IMPLEMENTING CHANGE

We were beginning to realize that under Marshall's new program our objectives in science were within reach. Conditions which we felt had kept us from reaching these goals were no longer imposed. Short periods, lack of preparation time, heterogeneous groupings of students, large classes, and similar rigidities became unnecessary under flexible scheduling, team teaching, and independent study. If the opportunity for a more effective educational program was within our power as teachers to provide, we now had the freedom to find the way in order that the changes in the behavior of our students would reflect more than ever before their participation in the science program.

The point had arrived when we were ready for dramatic and rapid change. What did it do to a teacher to be asked in a sincere manner, "How do you want to teach your course?" or, "How should it ideally be taught?" Some teachers reacted in disbelief to the newfound professional freedom. When the shock had worn off and the offer was still there, we started to plan as we had never before been able to do. We planned varied time blocks, different-sized groups, and reduced teacher-class contact time to allow for independent-study and conference time. Teachers formed teams to utilize varying competencies to greater advantage. We established a department office for more efficient use of teacher time, employed a science-department paraprofessional aide, opened up a subject-oriented resource center, and created open labs to add to the flexibility of our instructional patterns in many ways. We were given the responsibility to think big and to plan the most ideal program we could imagine for accomplishing the goals of each course.

Since the program—now a weekly cycle integrating all phases of each course—is reconstructed by the computer each year, we would have the opportunity to systematically evaluate the feedback and determine new course structures annually, utilizing the knowledge gained through the successes or failures we had experienced. This opportunity to observe and judge one's own program and then modify with new procedures the following year strangely and unfortunately was largely a unique experience for teachers. It might be considered a very real professional responsibility resulting in staff growth as well as in an improved program for students.

Team teaching, one innovational aspect of the metamorphosis in which we are engaged, has enabled us to try exciting, creative approaches to solve the many standard problems of teaching. In a sense we pulled the rug out from under ourselves and thus necessitated our rethinking both our philosophical position and our methods. Team teaching may be possible if the course's total enrollment is greater than the average class size. The goals of the course, the teaching-team members' strengths, and the physical arrangements within the building determine the pattern of large groups, laboratory, and small groups used. Teams within the science department typically deal with one subject at the present time, although during the fifth year one of the several interdisciplinary courses within the school involved a team from four departments including science. From the beginning of our new program, teams within the science department have been two-teacher teams with the assistance of the department aide. This teacher aide has charge of the science resource center, does much clerical work for the staff, and assists in the classroom in emergencies.

In the beginning the teaching teams were not organized by the department chairman or by the administrators. The teams developed through departmental planning to fulfill the need brought about by the demands of the students for courses. Team leaders were not appointed. But gradually as the team members planned and worked together, a leader emerged in each team. Time for planning sessions was set aside for all teachers in each team during the day by the computer, as a regular part of the weekly cycle. The individual obligations of the team members vary considerably; change from time to time; and tend to be determined by their own competencies and preferences, by the time each individual is willing and able to spend, and by the ideas and enthusiasm generated within the group.

A typical science course includes one or two large groups per weekly cycle. Large-group activities include lectures, films, demonstrations, guest speakers, and testing. The large group buys time for other parts of the program, such as small groups and individual student conferences. Attending the large group will be all the students enrolled in a particular course; this may be as many as 360 students. Laboratory activities are the type found in the programs described earlier. Each laboratory section is likely to be a medium-sized group of about twenty-five students. Emphasis in our program is placed on one or two laboratories per weekly cycle, from eighty to one hundred minutes each. Small groups of 13 to 15 students meet once a week for a period of forty minutes in most courses and provide time for student-to-student discussion. In the small group our teachers try to withdraw from the usual autocratic position to a place as a member of the group.

About one-third of each student's total school day is devoted to independent study, which we define as unstructured time, or as time during the school day when a student is not assigned to a class. During this time he may do work on assignments, make up work in open laboratories, tackle additional work of his own design, pursue recreational or self-directed reading, or go to the student union and just relax, having a snack and being sociable with his friends.

At the present time, programmed materials are being used only in the life science course, which has been designed by BSCS for the nonacademic learner in biology. Within the science department, we have the usual complement of science laboratories, which double as small-group rooms when not in use for actual laboratory work by a class. Large groups meet in either the auditorium or in double classrooms outside of the science area.

The science resource center mentioned earlier is essentially an expanded departmental library well equipped with reference and general reading materials in the sciences, including both books and periodicals. There are also some audio-visual aids, including filmstrips, 8-mm loop films, microfilms, tapes, and recordings. Adjacent to the science resource center, the science department office has facilitated a quantity and quality of communication among members of the department that was impossible or at least unlikely during the era of the self-contained classroom.

In general science at the ninth-grade level, we use two 40-minute large-group sessions each week, one 80-minute laboratory per week, and one 40-minute small-group meeting per week. The course is taught by a team of two teachers who plan together and share the responsibilities of large-group presentations and laboratory setups and instruction. The materials in this course cover primarily areas in the physical sciences. Immediately upon the completion of each topic within the course, the materials are rewritten to be used in their revised form the following year.

The academic biology course has used the Yellow Version BSCS materials since they were developed. This course has maintained a nearly stable structure of two 40-minute large-group meetings per week, one 100-minute laboratory session, and one 40-minute small group. In addition, there are several opportunities each week for students to come to an open lab for additional or makeup work. This course is taught by a team of two full-time biology teachers who have recently initiated as a part of their team offerings, but not as a part of the biology course, a study of laboratory techniques for a few very interested students who work on independent time with the teachers.

The nonacademic biology course, life science, has gone through an interesting evolution under modular-flexible scheduling. During its first year, the course structure was similar to the other biology course, using two large-group sessions, one lab, and one small group. Because it was readily apparent that these students benefited minimally from large-group presentations but did profit from activity-oriented classwork, large groups were cut to one per week and the labs increased to two per week, which also increased the total contact time between student and teacher. This schedule worked out very well. During the third year, an experimental program was inaugurated for this course in which one large group and one small group were maintained per week. However, the scheduled laboratory was abandoned in favor of a completely open-laboratory concept, in which students have the opportunity to come to the laboratory any time during their unstructured time for a period of two and a half days each week. This meant that students not only could come when they wished, with whom they wished, and as often as they wished, but also inherent was the choice not to come. This has been a very interesting experiment from which we feel we have found out many things about these students. During the fourth year, we retreated from the completely open-lab concept with these non-academically motivated students to a mixture of some scheduled-lab time for each student, plus open-laboratory time which he will need to finish his work. This has worked well and was continued the fifth year.

Chemistry and physics both have developed through a similar evolutionary process to the point where they now each have a large group per week, a small group or two per week, plus an open laboratory. The open lab with these self-directed students works out rather well. The comparison between the schedule that we now use and a traditional program was well stated by our chemistry teacher.

> I can teach the able students chemistry just as well with a traditional schedule, but if I am going to teach and the course is to encourage behavioral objectives—such as, responsibility for one's own learning, initiative, and behaving as a scientist behaves—in addition to chemistry subject matter, then I can do a better job of it with the flexible program.

Students of average and above-average ability and motivation find the program very exciting. They enjoy and utilize the freedom and accept the responsibility of the program well. These students are receiving excellent preparation in the budgeting of their time, which they report is very helpful in their education beyond high school. Some of them undoubtedly are learning more on their own time beyond class requirements than they would if they were forced to attend classes on a rigid traditional schedule.

The students with less academic ability or motivation find it difficult or are not interested in doing on their own much that teachers consider useful or appropriate. We are trying to design courses in each area of science that stress participation rather than listening for these low-achieving students. Many of these students learn very little through the traditional intellectual modes of communication, but they can and do learn material which their value system identifies as important both by doing and by discussing.

Each student's schedule allows ample time during which to have conferences with teachers if he so desires. This one-to-one meeting often has to be initiated by the teacher, although a student is free to make the appointment or to drop in at any time the teacher's program posted by the door shows unscheduled time that matches his.

ASSESSING THE NEW

From a teacher point of view, those of us in the science department are generally very happy with many of the aspects of the new program. We would not like to go back to the traditional fifty-five minute period, five-day-a-week schedule. The advantages we see in our new philosophy and structure are significant. Longer laboratory periods are extremely valuable. They make it possible to establish our purpose, get out materials, complete the project, clean up, and talk over our findings, all in one lab period of perhaps 100 minutes. This gives the student a far better opportunity to understand the significance of the work, and both he and the teacher gain a feeling of closure in regard to the topic. Valuable also is the freedom gained by the students to come in and make up work, go over work again, add to their work, and initiate ideas. The opportunity to have teacher-student conference time within the school day is helpful, especially in school-bus-route, low-student-interest, or high-student-employment areas. The freedom and relaxation experienced by the teacher in the new program is both productive and enjoyable. Each teacher has preparation time built into his schedule, which is particularly valuable to us in science, for lab preparations cannot be taken home. And the teacher-to-teacher contact, including the day-to-day critiques on each other's work, has helped us all to grow professionally. In planning with each other, we have the combined strength of at least two persons' ideas as well as their interaction, whereas formerly we had little more than our own individual ideas and textbooks to call upon. The variety in the program from day to day is stimulating in itself. Problems have not disappeared, but we feel we now have some new and better ways to attack them.

Evaluation of the program on an objective basis is very difficult. As scientists, we know that there are few, if any, bench marks from which to measure the success of the new techniques and methodologies. The feeling that each of us has for the success or failure of the program from a purely subjective point of view is probably the best evaluation we have at this time. As students leave our school and go into further education and into the world of work, we are getting and will continue to get comments from them as to the value of the new program they experienced at Marshall. Many hundreds of visitors, mostly educators, have come through our school in the last few years, and the evaluations made by these professionals after their visits are not to be neglected. Almost universally, they agree that we are on the right track, that we are working toward desirable goals; and teachers' and students' relative freedom from binding tension and inexorable frustration as we work toward more efficient ways to learn seems to liberate us and make us more open, more sensitive, and more perceptive.

In all our science courses, we are trying to work toward more subjective evaluations of behavioral objectives and away from strictly objective ratings of nonbehavioral objectives because we feel that a student's personal growth as well as his academic skills and comprehension are important. Formerly some teachers and students saw school success as predicated almost entirely on memorization and reflecting the teacher's academic postures, attitudes, and personal values. This often led to cheating and shallow conformity. Students often saw school as unreal and learning as unrelated to the problem solving required in the other aspects of their life. Teachers and students saw themselves as being on two teams. Teachers were working to tame students and show up their shortcomings. Students were endeavoring to get a grade the easiest way possible regardless of the education involved. Now the breakthrough in mechanics has also revolutionized methods and goals. Teamwork is catching on, for without the inflexible structure with its often repressive discipline, cooperation is not only more possible but also more necessary.

After five years, we are beginning to see the possibilities and obvious next steps in this kind of open schedule. With time I am sure we will continue to develop more and better ways to tap the full potential presented by this kind of program. I anticipate that additional parts of the sacred curriculum will be pared off and that both the teachers and students will find value in more and more independent-study and tutorial time. Undoubtedly independent research and study, short specialty courses, tutorials, and yet-to-be-discovered projects will carry credit toward graduation.

During the fourth year of our new design, a work-study program in horticulture, the use of greenhouses, and the biologic-economic aspects of nursery work was initiated at Marshall to a selected group of seniors who will then be prepared to step out into this vocation. More of this kind of vocational training and application of the classroom theory in work-study programs can be developed in connection with science and other disciplines.

As students become trained for independent work and become more responsible in the scheduling of their own time, I expect to see the use of more open laboratories in the science department as well as throughout the school. One of the most promising areas for development lies in an intramural VISTA (Volunteers in Service to America) or Peace Corps—enlisting scholastically superior or specially skilled students who feel a responsibility for, and satisfaction from, helping their fellow students. There is much research to show that students help themselves considerably academically and personally by helping each other. Meaningful involvement of any kind in the school program is also one of the best ways to generate on the part of the students a commitment to make that program work.

We all recognize the need in teaching for satisfaction and rewards beyond the paycheck. It is most stimulating to be recognized by your peers and superiors as a professional person, a person with professional responsibility, and an authority on how best to teach your particular subject. This is the atmosphere in which the teaching of science takes place at Marshall High School. We are free to experiment; we are encouraged to experiment. Not that we try new ideas just for the sake of trying things that are new, but because we are testing hypotheses that seem to be reasonable solutions to existing problems. Because we are scientists, we must experiment to establish new theories. Experimentation is the method at the heart of science. How can we test new ways of teaching other than by trying them out? Scientists and science teachers should be well equipped and more excited about the new designs in education than almost anyone else.

Try it! It is exciting to think about how you can improve your course content or method of instruction, to be free and able to design and to facilitate the improvement, and then to evaluate it and say to yourself, "It worked" or, "It didn't work."

Is there any better way to improve education?

9

Individualization of Learning Through Course Structures

William G. Tapfer

Computerized programming has allowed teachers to arrange the curriculum according to the way they want to teach it, the way students will benefit most. It has been said by many educators that flexible scheduling is a misnomer. In a sense this is true, depending on where flexibility is desired. If the wish is to change student and teacher schedules throughout the school year, computerized programming is not flexible. However, if the objective is to allow teachers the professional responsibility to design course structures in order to individualize instruction, the term is properly applied.

VARIABLE COURSE STRUCTURING

Too much flexibility can, in some instances, become an excuse for poor planning—too many "spur-of-the-moment decisions" with a tendency to forget about stated objectives. The flexibility of the Stanford School Scheduling System has allowed for individual teachers or teams of teachers and has given them the opportunity to design course structures according to individual needs. Typically, the schedule allows for large-group presentations, small-group discussions, laboratory periods of greater length, and the opportunity for independent study.

The time allocation for each class has traditionally been five meetings per week with forty-five to sixty minutes per period and with the number of students in each class between twenty-five and forty. With this lockstep structure, we find a restrictive situation.

First, we have assumed that the rate of learning is the same for all students; that students should participate in each course for an equal amount of time every day of the week. Have we considered basic objectives of each course when we structure courses in this manner? Should a course that has as one of its basic objectives the development of special skills be allocated the same amount of time as a course that is attempting to develop insights and understandings? Are all courses in the curriculum of equal importance to all children in their general high school education as far as allocation of time is concerned, or could some subjects be taught in a shorter length of time and others given additional time? These are major questions that have concerned educators for many years, but because of the convenience of the lockstep method of organizing the school day, very little has been done until recently to implement change.

Second, we ask ourselves what amount of recognition is being given to individual differences in the rate of learning. With the traditional method of structuring classes, we penalize a large percentage of students. Not only do we restrict the amount of time that a boy or girl can spend in attaining a degree of competency in a certain course, we also punish the accelerated student (and many times dampen his motivation) by requiring him to sit in class and wait for the student of average or low ability to attain some degree of proficiency in the subject matter being taught.

Not only do we have to be concerned with time allocation for the various activities, but also with class size. By the very nature of the activity, more efficiency and greater individualization of instruction can be attained if we are able to vary the class size according to need.

Third, we might ask ourselves whether we are making efficient use of the classroom teacher's time. The teacher who shows the same film to each of her classes for the entire day is certainly not using her time efficiently, but by the nature of the class structure, this is the only way that information contained in the film can reach each of her students. Also, the teacher has difficulty in locating high-caliber resource persons from the community to talk to her classes, for the competent person is usually too busy to spend the entire day speaking to five or six classes, and there is no way in a traditional program to bring these students together for a single presentation. With variable course structures, however, the large group lends itself to this type of activity. The same could be said of other activities that take place in the classroom which are beneficial to learning on the students' part but is wasting the time of the teacher.

These are but a few of the basic considerations which must be given to the educational process in our rapidly changing society. They are questions which were considered by the teachers in each of Marshall's twelve departments when they were asked one basic question, "How would you like to teach your courses next year without regard to the limitations of a conventional schedule?" The staff decided on a weekly cycle with an extended school day (8:05 A.M. to 3:15 P.M.) using a twenty-minute modular system consisting of twenty-one modules per day. They planned extensive use of teaching teams, large-group, lab, and small-group instructional periods, and independent-study time for students.

SCHEDULING TECHNIQUES

The planning for this type of variable course structure was made possible by the development of the Stanford School Scheduling System, the system used to generate the complex school master schedule and to assign students classes and classrooms after the master schedule has been determined.

Data is submitted by the school to the computer center on cards that have been keypunched locally. Basically, the information needed for computerized programming is general school parameters, course data, student course requests, teacher data, and room data. The Stanford School Scheduling System provides a manual which contains explicit instructions for submitting all necessary data.

It is obvious, of course, that certain parameters must be established for the teachers and departments planning their course structure. Excessive demands on the part of one or more departments can be highly restrictive and result in the generation of an unacceptable master program. The first program generated by SSSS for Marshall for the school year 1963–1964 was not an ideal program, but over a period of four years the staff of the school has had an opportunity for experimentation and the Stanford School Scheduling System has become more efficient in respect to building master programs.

Many changes have taken place each year in course structure; for example, group sizes have changed, time allocations for various phases of a course have been modified, open labs are used more extensively, and implementation of directed study has proved beneficial in some areas. It is through the use of computerized programming and modular-flexible scheduling that it is possible to make these changes from year to year and not have a static situation without regard for the individual students, teaching staff, and community.

The design of each course offered at Marshall is the result of careful planning by the teacher or team of teachers for the course. The teachers work closely with their department chairman and the administration in order to structure the course to match the needs of the students. The structure of each course will vary according to the ability of students enrolled in the course, the teacher, the nature of the subject being taught, and the activities involved in the course. As can be seen by examining the many courses offered, there is considerable difference in the structure of courses, and each is designed for a particular curriculum but is in keeping with the total school program.

The course structures are not presented in this chapter with the idea that they should be adopted in other schools but are given only as an example of the type of course structure one school has found most satisfactory, at one point in time, in an attempt to individualize instruction. When a new design is attempted, many factors must be considered such as the community, the students, teachers, the nature of the subject matter, and the educational philosophy of the school.

SIGNIFICANT TRENDS

The structure as seen for the 1966–1967 school year differs considerably from that of the first year of modular-flexible scheduling. This is due to the many experiences of the staff, exchange of ideas with other schools, new staff members, etc. It must also be said that computerized programming as a vehicle for instructional improvement has allowed for continual change. Teachers are no longer restricted by specific numbers of students in class or by the same length of time for each activity. They are now able to modify course structures from year to year.

Certain definite trends have been noted in the structure of classes over a four-year period of time. Small-group meetings have generally increased in time from forty minutes to one hour. It is the feeling on the part of many of the teachers that too often closure is not reached in forty minutes and that termination prior to closure by the majority of students is harmful to the learning process. Large-group meetings are usually held only once each week and are two modules, or forty minutes, in length. This seems to be the most ideal length of time to include most activities of a large group and still be within the attention span of most students. Certain teachers have, however, scheduled two large-group meetings per week or one large-group meeting of three modules. The maximum length of time for scheduled lab meetings is five modules, or 100 minutes. The attention span of the majority of students cannot go beyond this length of time, even in an activity area. Also, blocks of time greater than five modules become quite restrictive to the rest of the school program. After the first four years, it was fairly well established by the staff that open lab is educationally more sound than structured-lab time. This takes care of the individual differences. Those who need to work for many short periods of time during the week and those who find it much easier to work for long periods of time are both accommodated. Also, the amount of lab time spent per week is determined by the student. One individual may be able to accomplish the week's lab work in two hours, and other students may require as much as four hours or even more.

There has been a continual reduction in the number of medium groups within each course to the point that they have virtually disappeared. For years teachers have been accustomed to teaching groups of twenty-eight to thirty-five students, and so it stands to reason that it was difficult to change this pattern. The staff at Marshall has found there are only a very few activities in which medium groups are efficient. This size group is too large for any interaction on the part of the students, and so the teacher usually finds himself in the role of lecturer. If it is most profitable to lecture, this could be done just as effectively in a large-group setting with a great economy of time.

Low-ability youngsters are provided with more structured class time than those of average or above-average ability. Those students with limited ability usually need more encouragement and guidance from the teacher and so are given more class contact time and less unstructured time to work on their own.

These have been general observations and will not be true for all courses; for in the end, we find that each course is unique, as is each teacher and student.

MARSHALL COURSE STRUCTURES

The following pages provide the reader with explicit structures for the courses offered at Marshall High School during the school year 1966–1967. These course structures have undergone revision every year since the inception of modular-flexible scheduling; and the prognosis at this point is that course structures will continue to change as knowledge about learning increases, as physical facilities are adapted to the new design in education, and as teachers explore the wide range of possibilities encompassed in modular-flexible programming.

The following terms or abbreviations have been used in presenting all course structures in as concise a form as possible:

Course: This is the local school designation and is a group of one or more phases that is identifiable by the curricular content. The course is identified in parentheses. The use of A, B, or C indicates ability-level grouping, with A the highest.

Phase ID: The identification of the element of the course structure, which has a definite length, a meeting time, size, or purpose.

LG: Large group (45 to 400 students)

MG: Medium group (16 to 45 students)

SG: Small group (6 to 15 students)

LAB: Laboratory (12 to 32 students)

COMP: Lab designed specifically for development of composition skills (30 to 60 students)

PPM: Periods, or modules, per meeting.

MPW: Meetings per week.

The real revolution in education that has taken place at Marshall and other schools throughout the nation which are involved in flexible programming is not simply in organizational patterns or modular scheduling. These are obvious manifestations of the really significant change—a desire to focus the mechanics of a school schedule on meaningful learning experiences, to create a learning-oriented school program, to allow teachers to create programs specifically designed for their students and curriculum.

A close analysis of the following course structures demonstrates individualization that has never before been possible with a traditional system. Included in each course are phases specifically designed for the learning activity that takes place, as determined by the teacher or team of teachers involved.

Course Structures Marshall High School 1966–1967

Course	*Phase ID*	*PPM*	*MPW*	*No. sec.*	*Teachers per sec.*	*Sec. size*	*Special features*
E 1-2A-B (Freshman English)	LG	3	1	4	2	125	Master course
	COMP	3	1	12	1	42	
	SG	2	2	36	1	14	
SS 1-2A-B (Freshman Social Studies)	LAB	3	1	12	1	42	All students meet
	SG	2	2	36	1	14	with E 1-2A-B LG
ESS 1-2C (Freshman English & Social Studies)	MG	4	4	3	2	41	All students must also take ES 1
E 3-4EE (Sophomore English)	SG	2	2	1	1	16	All students meet with E 3-4A LG
E 3-4A (Sophomore English)	LG	2	1	1	2	81	All students must
	LAB	4	1	6	1	27	also take E 3 AS
	SG	2	2	12	1	14	
E 3-AS (Rhetoric)	LG	2	1	1	1	153	
	SG	3	1	9	1	17	
E 3-4B (Sophomore English)	LG	2	1	1	4	270	
	LAB	3	2	10	1	27	
	SG	2	1	20	1	14	
E 3-4C (Sophomore English)	LG	2	1	1	2	105	
	LAB	4	1	4	1	26	
	MG	2	2	4	1	26	
	SG	2	1	8	1	13	

Course	Phase ID	PPM	MPW	No. sec.	Teachers per sec.	Sec. size	Special features
E 5-6A (Junior English)	LG	2	1	2	2	117	
	LAB	4	1	4	1	29	
	SG	3	1	8	1	15	
	SG	2	1	8	1	15	
E 5-6B (Junior English)	LG	2	1	1	3	305	
	LAB	3	2	10	1	31	
	SG	2	1	20	1	15	
E 5-6C (Junior English)	LAB	3	3	3	1	32	
	SG	2	2	6	1	16	
E 7-8EE (Senior English)	LAB	3	1	1	1	15	All students meet
	SG	2	1	1	1	15	with E 7-8A LG
E 7-8A (Senior English)	LG	2	1	1	2	142	Master course
	LAB	3	2	5	1	28	
	SG	2	1	10	1	14	
E 7-8B (Senior English)	LG	2	1	1	3	263	
	LAB	4	1	10	1	26	
	SG	2	2	20	1	13	
E 7-8C (Senior English)	LAB	3	3	4	1	24	
	SG	2	1	8	1	12	
EV 3-8 (Vocational English)		2	3	1	2	36	Must be enrolled in IM 1-2
		2	2	1	2	36	or IPD 1-2–"C" ability-non-graded
ES 1 (Speech–½ unit)	MG	2	2	4	1	31	Must be enrolled in
	SG	2	1	8	1	15	ESS 1-2C

Course	*Phase ID*	*PPM*	*MPW*	*No. sec.*	*Teachers per sec.*	*Sec. size*	*Special features*
ES 1-2 (Speech)	LG	2	1	1	3	133	
	MG	2	1	4	1	33	
	SG	3	2	8	1	16	
ES 3-8 (Advanced Speech)	LG	2	1	1	2	64	3 modules of directed study
	MG	2	1	2	1	32	
	SG	3	1	4	1	16	
ED 1-2 (Dramatics)	LG	2	2	1	1	54	
	SG	3	2	3	1	18	
ED 3-4 (Advanced Dramatics)	SG	3	3	1	1	16	Open lab
IS 1-2 (Stagecraft)	SG	3	2	1	1	10	Open lab
EJ 1-2 (Beginning Journalism)	MG	3	2	2	1	19	Open lab
	SG	2	2	4	1	10	
EJ 3-4 (Advanced Journalism)	LAB	4	1	1	1	12	Open lab
	SG	2	3	1	1	12	
EP 1-2 (Student Publications)	LAB	4	1	1	1	23	Open lab
	MG	3	3	1	1	23	
EER 1 (Effective Reading)	LG	2	1	1	1	71	
	SG	2	2	4	1	17	
ELS 1-2 (Library Science)	SG	2	1	1	1	12	10 modules of directed study
SS 5-6A (American History)	LG	2	2	2	4	206	Master course
	SG	2	3	27	1	15	

Course	Phase ID	PPM	MPW	No. sec.	Teachers per sec.	Sec. size	Special features
SS 5-6B (American History)	MG	2	3	4	2	25	All students meet with SS 5-6A LG
SS 7-8A (American Problems)	LG	2	2	2	4	185	Master course
	SG	3	2	24	1	15	
SS 7-8B (American Problems)	SG	2	3	6	1	16	All students meet with SS 7-8A LG
SS 7-8EE (American Problems)	SG	3	2	1	1	18	Open lab
SS 3 (World History–½ unit)	SG	3	2	3	1	16	
SS 9-10 R (Russian Soviet History)	SG	3	2	2	1	13	
SS 11 (Intro. to Psychology & Sociology–½ unit)	SG	3	2	6	1	20	
M 1-2 (General Math)	MG	2	2	6	1	30	
	MG	3	2	6	1	30	
M 3-4 (General Math)	MG	2	2	2	1	24	
	MG	3	2	2	1	24	
MIA 1-2 (Intro. to Algebra)	MG	3	4	5	1	28	
MA 1-2 (Algebra)	LG	3	1	2	1	88	Open lab
	MG	3	1	6	1	33	
	MG	2	3	6	1	33	
MIA 1-2 (Intro. to Algebra)	LG	3	2	2	1	90	Open lab
MIA 3-4 (Intro. to Algebra 2nd year)	LG	2	1	1	1	129	
	MG	2	2	5	1	25	
	LAB	2	2	5	1	25	

Course	Phase ID	PPM	MPW	No. sec.	Teachers per sec.	Sec. size	Special features
MA 3-4 (Algebra)	LG	3	1	1	1	83	
	MG	3	1	3	1	28	
	MG	2	3	3	1	28	
MG 1-2 (Geometry)	LG	3	1	2	1	90	
	MG	2	3	6	1	30	
	LAB	3	1	3	1	30	
MS 1-2 (Senior Math)	LG	3	2	1	1	38	Open lab
MS 3-4 (Math–fifth year)	MG	3	4	1	1	12	
MC 1-2 (Consumer Math)	LG	2	1	1	1	128	
	MG	3	2	4	1	32	
	MG	2	1	4	1	32	
MR 1-2 (Refresher Math)	MG	2	2	2	1	99	
	MG	3	2	2	1	50	
SG 1-2 (General Science)	LG	2	2	1	3	329	4 modules of directed study
	LAB	4	1	12	1	27	
	SG	2	1	24	1	14	
SB 1-2L (Life Science)	LG	3	1	1	1	131	Open lab
	LAB	4	1	6	1	22	
	SG	2	1	12	1	11	
SB 1-2 (BSCS Biology)	LG	2	2	1	2	304	4 modules of directed study
	LAB	5	1	12	1	25	
	SG	2	1	24	1	13	

Course	*Phase ID*	*PPM*	*MPW*	*No. sec.*	*Teachers per sec.*	*Sec. size*	*Special features*
SC 1-2 (Chemistry)	LG	3	1	1	1	105	Open lab
	LG	2	1	1	1	105	
	LAB	3	2	6	1	17	
SP 1-2 (Physics)	LAB	3	4	1	1	19	Open lab
SPS 1-2 (Physical Science)	LG	2	1	1	1	77	3 modules of directed study
	LAB	3	1	4	1	19	
	SG	2	2	4	1	19	
SPh 1-2 (Physiology)	LG	2	1	1	1	18	Open lab
	LAB	3	3	1	1	18	
SR 1-2 (Science Research)		2	1	1	1	14	Open lab
SNE 3-8 (Horticulture)		9	5	1	1	25	½ day work experience
L 1-2 (Latin–first year)	MG	3	4	1	1	20	Open lab
	LAB	1	1	1	1	20	
L 3-4 (Latin–second year)	LG	2	1	1	1	29	Open lab
	SG	2	4	2	1	15	
	LAB	1	1	1	1	29	
S 1-2 (Spanish–first year)	LG	2	1	1	2	76	Open lab
	MG	2	4	4	1	19	
	LAB	1	2	3	1	25	
S 3-4 (Spanish–second year)	LG	2	1	1	1	46	Open lab
	MG	2	4	2	1	23	
	LAB	1	2	2	1	23	

Course	*Phase ID*	*PPM*	*MPW*	*No. sec.*	*Teachers per sec.*	*Sec. size*	*Special features*
S 5-6 (Spanish–third year)	MG	3	1	1	1	21	Open lab
	MG	2	3	1	1	21	
	LAB	1	1	1	1	21	
F 1-2 (French–first year)	LG	2	1	1	2	104	Open lab
	MG	2	4	5	1	21	
	LAB	1	2	4	1	26	
F 3-4 (French–second year)	LG	2	1	1	1	66	Open lab
	MG	2	4	3	1	22	
	LAB	1	2	3	1	22	
F 5-6 (French–third year)	MG	3	1	1	1	24	Open lab
	MG	2	3	1	1	24	
	LAB	1	2	1	1	24	
F 7-8 (French–fourth year)	MG	2	4	1	1	11	Open lab
	LAB	1	2	1	1	11	
G 1-2 (German–first year)	LG	2	1	1	2	120	Open lab
	SG	2	4	5	1	24	
	LAB	1	2	5	1	24	
G 3-4 (German–second year)	LG	2	1	2	2	96	Open lab
	MG	2	4	4	1	24	
	LAB	1	2	4	1	24	
G 5-6 (German–third year)	MG	3	1	1	1	20	Open lab
	MG	2	3	1	1	20	
	LAB	1	1	1	1	20	

Course	*Phase ID*	*PPM*	*MPW*	*No. sec.*	*Teachers per sec.*	*Sec. size*	*Special features*
G 7-8 (German–fourth year)	MG	3	2	1	1	12	Open lab
	MG	2	2	1	1	12	
	LAB	1	1	1	1	12	
BT 1 (Typing–½ unit)	MG	2	3	12	1	43	
BT 2 (Typing–½ unit)	MG	2	3	3	1	34	
BT 2-3 (Advanced Typing)	MG	3	3	4	1	37	
	MG	2	1	4	1	37	
BR 1 (Recordkeeping–½ unit)	MG	2	3	4	1	30	
BBh 1 (Briefhand–½ unit)	MG	2	3	4	1	29	
BS 1-2 (Shorthand)	MG	3	3	3	1	28	
	MG	2	1	3	1	28	
BS 3-4 (Advanced Shorthand)	MG	3	3	2	1	21	
	MG	2	1	2	1	21	
BG 1-2 (General Business)	LG	2	1	1	2	193	Master course
	SG	2	3	9	1	21	
BG 1-2B (General Business)	SG	2	3	3	1	17	All students meet with BG 1-2 LG
BB 1-2 (Bookkeeping)	MG	3	2	4	1	30	
	MG	3	1	4	1	30	
	MG	2	1	4	1	30	
BL 1-2 (Business Law)	LG	2	1	1	1	111	
	SG	2	3	6	1	19	

Course	*Phase ID*	*PPM*	*MPW*	*No. sec.*	*Teachers per sec.*	*Sec. size*	*Special features*
BOP 1-2 (Business Office Practice)	LG	2	1	1	1	80	
	MG	2	4	4	1	20	
BDE 1-2 (Distributive Education)	JOB	6	5	1	1	94	Work experience
	LG	2	1	1	1	94	modules 16-21
	MG	2	4	3	1	32	
BOA 1-2 (Office Assistant)	MG	1	1	2	1	18	12 modules directed study
PE 1-2B (Boys' Physical Ed.)	LAB	4	2	8	1	30	
	LAB	3	1	8	1	30	
PE 3-4B (Boys' Physical Ed.–½ unit)	LAB	3	3	8	1	34	
PE 3-4 HB (Boys' Health–½ unit)	LG	2	1	2	3	137	
	MG	3	1	10	1	27	
PE 1-2G (Girls' Physical Ed.)	LAB	4	2	8	1	39	
	LAB	3	1	8	1	39	
PE 3-4 (Girls' Physical Ed.–½ unit)	LAB	3	3	8	1	35	
PE 3-4 (Girls' Health–½ unit)	LG	2	1	2	2	141	
	SG	3	1	12	1	24	
PE 5-6B (Boys' Physical Ed.)	LAB	3	2	1	1	34	
	LAB	4	1	1	1	34	
PE 7-8B (Boys' Physical Ed.)	LAB	1	2	2	1	43	Directed study
PE 5-6G (Girls' Physical Ed.)	LAB	3	2	1	1	21	
	LAB	4	1	1	1	21	
PE 7-8G (Girls' Physical Ed.)	LAB	1	2	1	1	9	Directed study

Course	Phase ID	PPM	MPW	No. sec.	Teachers per sec.	Sec. size	Special features
MUC 1-2B (Beginning Chorus–boys)	MG	3	2	1	1	25	
	MG	2	2	1	1	25	
MUC 1-2G (Beginning Chorus–girls)	MG	3	2	1	1	34	
	MG	2	2	1	1	34	
MUC 3-8G (Girls' Senior Choir)	MG	3	2	1	1	34	
	MG	2	2	1	1	34	
MUC 3-8 (Advanced Choir)	LG	3	2	1	1	73	Meet mods. 2-4 Wed. &
	LG	2	1	1	1	73	Fri.–master course
MUC 3-8 M (Advanced Male Choir)	MG	3	1	1	1	26	Must also take MUC 3-8
MUC 3-8 F (Advanced Female Choir)	MG	3	1	1	1	41	Must also take MUC 3-8
MuU 1 (Music Understanding–½ unit)	MG	2	3	1	1	2	
MuEn 1 (Music Ensemble–½ unit)	MG	3	2	1	1	14	
MuOB 1-2 (Beginning Band and Orchestra)	MG	2	1	1	1	7	Must also take MuB 3-4
MuB 3-4 (Intermediate Band)	MG	3	2	1	1	26	Master course
	MG	3	1	1	1	26	
MuB 3-4 WW (Woodwinds)	SG	3	1	1	1	10	Must also take MuB 3-4
MuB 3-4B (Brass)	SG	3	1	1	1	16	Must also take MuB 3-4
MuB 5-8 (Advanced Band)	LG	3	2	1	1	85	Meet mods 2-4 Wed. &
	LG	3	1	1	1	85	Fri.– Master Course
MuB 5-8 WW (Woodwinds)	SG	3	1	2	1	20	Must also take MuB 3-4
MuB 5-8 HB (High Brass)	SG	3	1	1	1	30	Must also take MuB 3-4

Course	*Phase ID*	*PPM*	*MPW*	*No. sec.*	*Teachers per sec.*	*Sec. size*	*Special features*
MuB 5-8 LBP (Low Brass–Percussion)	SG	3	1	1	1	35	Must also take MuB 3-4
MuO 3-8 (Orchestra)	LG	3	2	1	1	37	Master course
	LG	4	1	1	1	37	
MuO 3-8V (Violin)	LAB	3	1	1	1	21	Must also take MuO 3-8
MuO VCB (Viola–Cello–Bass)	LAB	3	1	1	1	16	Must also take MuO 3-8
AG 1-2 (General Art)	LAB	4	2	7	1	26	
	LAB	3	1	7	1	26	
AG 1-2S (Art–General for Juniors and Seniors)	LAB	4	1	2	1	23	3 modules of
	LAB	4	1	2	1	23	directed study
AG 3-8 (Art General–Advanced)	LAB	4	1	4	1	28	Open lab
	LAB	4	1	4	1	28	
AM 1-2 (Art Metal)	LAB	3	2	2	1	22	4 modules of directed study
Au 1 (Art Understanding–½ unit)	LAB	3	2	1	1	15	
AL 1 (Art Lettering–½ unit)	LAB	3	2	3	1	25	
ACC 1-2 (Ceramics)	LAB	3	1	3	1	24	4 modules of directed study
	LAB	3	1	3	1	24	
ACC 3-4 (Ceramics)	LAB	3	2	2	1	18	Open lab
AS 1-2 (Art Staff)	LAB	3	2	1	1	7	Open lab
AC 1-2 (Crafts)	LAB	3	3	1	1	27	

Course	Phase ID	PPM	MPW	No. sec.	Teachers per sec.	Sec. size	Special features
IA 1-2 (Intro. to Industrial Arts)	LG	2	1	1	4	160	
	LAB	4	2	2	2	40	
	IL	2	1	2	2	40	
IW 1-2 (Basic Woodwork)	LAB	4	1	2	1	26	Must take IA 3-4
	IL	2	1	2	1	26	4 mods. directed study
IW 3-4 (Woodwork–Advanced)	LAB	4	1	2	1	12	Must take IA 5-6
	IL	2	1	2	1	12	Open lab
IM 1-2 (Basic Metalwork)	LAB	4	1	2	1	16	Must take IA 3-4
	IL	2	1	2	1	16	4 mods. directed study
IM 3-4 (Advanced Metalwork)	LAB	4	1	2	1	16	Must take IA 5-6
	IL	2	1	2	1	16	open lab
IE 1-2 (Basic Electronics)	LAB	4	1	2	1	18	Must take IA 3-4
	IL	2	1	1	1	37	4 mods. directed study
IE 3-4 (Advanced Electronics)	LAB	4	1	1	1	25	Must take IA 5-6
	IL	2	1	1	1	25	open lab
IPD 1-2 (Production Drafting)	LAB	4	1	2	1	26	Must take IA 3-4
	IL	2	1	2	1	26	4 mods. directed study
IAD 3-4 (Architectural and Structural Drafting)	LAB	4	1	2	1	17	Must take IA 5-6
	IL	2	1	2	1	17	open lab
IED 5-6 (Engineering Drafting Problems)	LAB	4	1	1	1	9	Must take IA 5-6
	IL	2	1	1	1	9	open lab
IA 3-4 (Large group for Advanced Industrial Arts)	LG	2	1	1	4	178	

Course	Phase ID	PPM	MPW	No. sec.	Teachers per sec.	Sec. size	Special features
IA 5-6 (Large group for Advanced Industrial Arts)	LG	2	1	1	4	123	
H 1-2 (Beginning Home Economics)	LG	2	1	1	3	118	
	LAB	3	1	5	1	24	
	LAB	4	1	5	1	24	
	SG	2	1	10	1	12	
H 3-4 (Home Economics–second year)	LG	2	1	1	1	53	
	LAB	3	1	2	1	26	
	LAB	4	1	2	1	26	
	SG	2	1	4	1	13	
H 3-4s (Home Economics for Sophomores, Juniors, and Seniors)	LAB	3	1	1	1	28	Open lab
	LAB	4	1	1	1	28	
	SG	2	1	2	1	14	
H 5-6 (Home Economics–third year)	LG	2	1	1	1	70	
	LAB	4	1	3	1	24	Open lab
	SG	2	1	6	1	12	
H 7-8 (Home Economics–fourth year)	LAB	4	1	1	1	25	All students meet with H 7-8 c LG
	SG	2	1	2	1	13	Open lab
H 7-8c (Cooperative Homemaking–Family Living–Coed)	LG	2	1	1	2	106	Master course
	LAB	3	1	4	2	20	
	LAB	4	1	4	2	20	
	SG	2	1	8	1	10	

Course	*Phase ID*	*PPM*	*MPW*	*No. sec.*	*Teachers per sec.*	*Sec. size*	*Special features*
H 7-8s (Clothing Construction)	LG	2	1	1	1	31	Open lab
	LAB	3	3	2	1	15	
H 7s (Clothing Construction–½ unit)	LAB	3	2	1	1	13	

The method used at Marshall for designing course structure has been to directly involve the teacher or team of teachers who will be instructing the course. They work closely with their department chairman and the administrative staff in designing course structure that not only has sound educational rationale but will fit into the total school program.

Examples of the difference in course structure may be noted by examining courses within each department and relating this structure to the general activities that take place within each subject.

English and social studies on the freshman level is a combined area and employs team teaching for all ability levels. A difference in structure may be noted between the average- and above-average-ability youngsters (A and B) as compared to those of low ability (C track). It has been the opinion of the teachers who have been involved over a four-year period of time that low-ability students benefit less from large-group instruction, consequently large group has been eliminated for the low-ability freshmen in English and social studies. They now meet four days a week for a greater period of time. This allows the teachers to work more closely with the class and to direct the learning activities. By structuring in this way, students of low ability will have less unstructured time during the week than those with average or above-average ability.

An analysis of the structure of each of the courses offered in the English department shows a great deal of individuality. Consideration has been given to the ability level of the students involved as well as the activity that takes place in each level of English. Also, the teachers or teaching teams have structured the course according to their method of presentation. As an example, the sophomore team of English A was concerned about the writing preparation on the part of the students. Test scores indicated these students were relatively low in this area of language arts. One of the major concerns was to improve writing abilities; consequently one writing lab per week was designed for the course structure. This is in addition to large-group instruction and small-group learning situations. The teaching team in senior English decided on two lab meetings per week but of only one-hour duration. This is pointed out in an attempt to show an individualization in course structure on the part of the teachers. Rationale for the teaching of English is explained in detail in a previous chapter.

By the nature of the subject, social studies allows for more large-group presentation than most other subjects in the curriculum. A great deal of use is made of the lecture method, film presentation, and resource persons. Consequently, the social studies teachers feel that two large groups per week are necessary. Most other areas of the curriculum have only one large-group meeting per week.

Course structure in the area of mathematics is quite diverse. A small portion of the staff feels more comfortable in a teaching situation which approximates the former traditional program; the rest of the math staff has experienced success with the team and math lab approach.

Occasionally, as in the case of MIA 1–2 (Introduction to Algebra), two entirely different structures of the same course may be found. In this particular course it will be noted that two teachers each have their own classes which meet four days a week, and the other two teachers have teamed for two large-group presentations per week and in addition conduct an open math lab. This lab provides the student with the opportunity for individual assistance throughout the week. Students participating in this math lab will not only find the two math teachers but also senior math students who are scheduled to the math lab and are available to provide assistance.

As we analyze the many course offerings in science, we find a variety of structures. The trend, not only in science but in most lab subjects, is that a generous amount of structure be given to students of the lower grades and less structure as we approach the upper level. Science makes good use of the open-lab concept; that is, students are "assigned" for a minimum amount of time but participate in open lab during their unstructured time. Science teachers have experimented a great deal in attempting to find a suitable structure for each of the courses. They have gone from an extreme during the first year of having all lab work scheduled, to the other end of the continuum during the 1965–1966 school year when one course met formally for only one hour per week. It was found that a compromise somewhere between the two extremes suited the needs of the majority of students. Science has been discussed in more detail in a preceding chapter.

Foreign language is one area of the curriculum where a continuing need is found by the teachers for a standard-size class (medium group). Language teachers at Marshall High School seem to feel that in the area of foreign language a student should meet as many times per week as possible in the same group. Language lab is separated from the normal structure and is usually assigned for two 1-module meetings per week. Students, however, are encouraged to make use of the language lab at least once each day. This is on an open-lab basis.

A variety of course structures will be found in business education according to the needs of the particular subject. Typing, for example, may be taught just as effectively in a large-group situation as in a small group, whereas general business may be more effectively learned in small-group situations.

Physical education is required only during the freshman and sophomore years at Marshall High School. A class for selected students is offered on the junior and senior level. Students are not structured into class each day of the week in P.E. but have an opportunity to participate in an open-lab situation.

Band and choir are the most restrictive of the general course offerings, not only in a modular schedule but also in a traditional program. Some priority has been given to this area to provide them with the most ideal situation possible. For example, advanced band and advanced choir have been given a time-pattern specification so that they meet following an extended registration period (this usually follows an assembly). In addition to the large-group meetings at a specified time, small groups have been designed for various instrumental groupings.

Art has undergone a considerable change in structure in each of the past five years. Teachers have tried large-group instruction, extensive open lab, and maximum structure. The preceding listing of course structures shows that those students participating in an art course for the first time are given considerable structure and those who are engaged in advanced courses are given less structure with more open-lab time.

Four industrial arts teachers have teamed for large-group presentations in the area of industrial arts. The emphasis in the large group is on the dissemination of occupational information. Instructional lab (IL) is used for demonstrations and/or discussion purposes. Lab is utilized for the development of manual skills. More structure is given to first-year students, as was the case in art, and less structure to advanced students.

Home economics, like other lab subjects, has provided maximum structure for first-year students and has relied upon the open lab for students in advanced courses.

Each discipline at Marshall High School has been discussed very briefly, not to provide a complete rationale in each of the subject-matter areas, but to point out the individualization that is possible in a modular-flexible schedule. Courses are constructed with consideration being given to the size of the class, to the number of class meetings per week, to the length of class meetings, to the characteristics of the students involved, and to the professional opinion of the teachers who are responsible for teaching the course.

10

The Guidance Program and Student Activities

Rose B. Coffman

THE GUIDANCE PROGRAM

The role of the counselor, like that of the classroom teacher, has changed in the five years of modular-flexible scheduling at John Marshall High School. It has become one of greater importance, more so than the counselors perceive as yet. Theirs is the awesome responsibility of helping the student realize his full potential in his course of study, choice of college or work, and even his everyday behavior as he tries to understand success and failure. One can say that this is so regardless of the kind of program the child has—and this is true. But only in a program similar to Marshall's is the child on independent time from 20 to 50 percent of his school week and thereby free to choose how he will use this time. Implications for counseling in such an environment are apparent. Moreover this also means that an ever-increasing number of students seek their counselors, as both student and counselor are now more available to each other. Students who participate in athletics, who have family responsibilities, or who have part-time jobs can find time to see their counselors during the school day. No one could foresee, before we entered our modular program, how vitally involved the counseling services would become.

As classroom teachers met to discuss their views of the new structure for their courses, counselors took part and became involved and eager, but concerned. The new program appeared to offer much for everyone, except the counselors. As had been the Portland policy, our counselors were only part-time in the counseling office and spent the remainder of the day in the classroom. As is usually true, they were good teachers and, in this role, most interested in being a part of team teaching and modular scheduling. The amount of counseling time was the same as in the traditional system. It was envisioned that the counselor's "independent time" would provide more modules for counseling—only counselors had no independent time as did the teaching staff and the students.

The first year the administration decided that the counselors should spend as much time as needed to help with the teaching program. As teachers, they needed to attend team meetings, take part in and observe large groups, and learn (with the faculty) the intricacies of small-group techniques. As was true with the teachers, class preparation had to be planned and papers corrected. And so a conflict developed. Counselors found themselves in a dynamic teaching experience with a dedicated faculty on one side and an increased responsibility to the same faculty and their counselees on the other.

With the counselor-student ratio the same and with counselors teaching the equivalent of one or two classes, depending upon the number of counselees and *extra* responsibilities assigned (vocational, testing, college), it was felt that more time was needed if counselors were to know and work effectively with their counselees. Long before the year ended, it was evident that with Marshall's plan of flexible scheduling, some changes had to be made—discussion of full-time counseling was the topic of the day at counselors' meetings.

During the second year adjustments were made, but counselors still taught the equivalent of a class or two. Counselors still enjoyed being a part of the new teaching program, even though there was not enough time to meet the ever-increasing demands on the counseling department. The counseling chairman, who had had full-time counseling for two years, realized that as the liaison and coordinating person for the entire staff he had little time to meet with his counselees. His office was a hub of activity. Program changes and course deletions and additions came through the administration to him. Class loads, teacher requests, and department complaints of any description were channeled through his office. Everything seemed to have top priority. The demands could not be met successfully until the structure of the counseling department became as streamlined as the rest of the Marshall program.

It was decided that as long as change was inevitable, Marshall would continue its policy of trying to find a more effective way to serve the community through the counseling services. Full-time counseling for seven counselors was planned for the following year. Each counselor would be working with both boys and girls, and vertical counseling (ninth to twelfth grade) would be adopted; that is, each counselor would have approximately one-seventh of each of the four classes as his counseling assignment. Although this plan is not new in counseling department organization, some trepidation was felt by several of our counselors who were accustomed to having only their own sex for counselees. Even so, all were eager to try. After a year of the new organization, no one wanted to return to the former organizational plan. As is always true, there are advantages and disadvantages in the present system. The plus factors far outweigh the minus ones, however.

Each counselor must be familiar with the entire school program. All must be conversant with college and vocational developments and opportunities. Seven counselors write college and job recommendations instead of the usual two. The Marshall community is a transient one; students come and leave at the rate of approximately three hundred per year. Most new students are freshmen and sophomores, probably because families tend to move less frequently after their children have roots in a school and bring pressure to stay to graduate with their classmates. It helps to have the new students distributed among all the counselors.

All contact with the classroom and with the teaching staff was not lost under the new organization. Counselors have discovered that their special strengths and interests can be utilized by the classroom teacher, thus maintaining another link between the teachers and the counselors. With full-time counseling, it is imperative for the counselor to keep alive the feeling of achievement or the need for help that all classroom teachers experience in their everyday teaching. Thus when counselors are invited to participate in a large-group presentation or when they are asked to view a film or to visit a small-group discussion, or even to take their share of supervision, they have responded and have found "the keeping in touch" gives them a continuing realistic picture of the school program. One counselor remarked that he had almost forgotten the difference in the caliber of students in the general math class as compared to the same age group in an algebra class. One morning's teaching experience was an instant "refresher." Another counselor after visiting an art class with the express purpose of asking to have "just one more student enrolled in her class" returned to the counseling office with the comment, "She already has thirty and that's more than she has teaching stations. Besides you should see some of the kids she has, and their level of interest. There is no doubt she has reached her limit in numbers for that class." Another counselor, after an invitation to help in the effective reading class, returned with the remark that she had forgotten how truly exciting it can be to teach.

Marshall's program also provides the opportunity for counselors to observe a counselee as he is with his peers in a small group or in any classroom situation. Our faculty and students have become so accustomed to visitors that neither is disturbed by visitors from our own staff. At first counselors expressed fear that teachers would envision any classroom visitation as an intrusion, but they soon discovered that teachers welcomed, and sometimes invited, their observing students for whom they wanted help.

Counselees, quite naturally, usually present only their side when they are involved in an unhappy classroom experience. It is also fair to say that, at least in the first interview, this viewpoint is slanted in favor of the counselee. Since teachers at Marshall have unstructured time the same as students, it is possible to arrange conferences with the student and his teacher during the school day. A conference skillfully handled can result in better understanding and a glimpse of insight into the teacher-student relationship that can be beneficial to all concerned. A mature counselor who can be helpful, but objective; understanding, but not emotionally involved; a listener, but not a lecturer can do much toward helping both teacher and student to develop an awareness of the real feelings that exist in all classroom situations.

Counselors with special responsibilities have found the teachers are responsive when requests are made to speak to their large groups concerning college visits, testing arrangements, and vocational opportunities. This is a distinct advantage and "time saver" because students have large-group meetings in which audio-visual aids are available; and the presentation need be made only once, in contrast to a traditional system in which the same presentation has to be given many times.

For the past two years, we have assigned a specific counselor to each of our feeder schools. No counselor has more than two elementary schools and all are at liberty to work out a schedule for contacting the school principal and his eighth-grade teachers. If the elementary school requests, our counselors will meet with the students and their parents for individual conferences. When invited, they go to the school to explain and discuss our unique program. Elementary school principals and teachers have reacted enthusiastically to this plan. Since our counselors are full time, it is not difficult to arrange a meeting that is convenient for the elementary schools.

For several years the counselors have been experimenting with the possibilities and limitations of group guidance. We began with groups of ten to fifteen on the freshman level. The selection was made from those students who had independent-study modules at the same time. It was felt all freshmen had questions they wanted to explore about school, dress, clubs, dances, and the like. It was hoped that from such discussions some real interaction would emerge about their feelings concerning problems that were important to them. Students with like problems of some magnitude could then be scheduled into very small groups for group counseling sessions.

However, no counselor has successfully kept a group going past the "information stages." We still feel that much can be accomplished in groups of freshmen for guidance purposes but that groups for counseling should be smaller and selected, perhaps, with more common concerns.

Counselors, too, need more help in group work if they are to be effective. It is our hope that we will be able to secure resource persons from the district who can help in this training.

Teachers have begun to ask for the use of the case study in an effort to understand more thoroughly certain teen-agers who have special handicaps or emotional problems. In one example a teacher of a totally blind freshman girl has asked that all her teachers have a session with the counselor, her Braille teacher, and anyone else who works with her to discuss problems and successes they have had with her. In another typical example, the social worker, the counselor, and the teachers of an emotionally disturbed student met to discuss ways of keeping the child in school. Teachers gain much from such a conference, and counselors get genuine insight into the everyday problems the teachers meet with such a student. We find it is very worthwhile to share and gain different approaches to cope with problems involved in trying to help the disturbed student remain in school.

The beginning of the third year of the new design, we instituted a full-time vocational counselor. Because 50 percent of our students will enter the world of work as soon as they graduate, the vocational aspect of the counseling program is of marked importance. It is the responsibility of the vocational counselor to work with the various departments to deliver large-group presentations relative to vocational opportunities arising from the various subject fields. He also arranges field trips, so that the students become aware of the qualifications necessary for specific jobs and the preparation needed for various job clusters. Our vocational counselor is working most effectively with the classroom teacher in arranging resource persons for large-group presentations and in making conference time available for students who have independent time following the class presentation. He has been successful, especially, with the representatives from the apprenticeship council, military groups, and vocational-college people.

Our vocational counselor has discovered that flexible scheduling is conducive to *mass* participation for demonstrations, lectures, and conferences arranged by business and college groups. Each year he has had a number of displays brought into the school by business and industry. A good example is the telephone-company display set up in the main hall, a demonstration using equipment similar to that found at various industry fairs. Hundreds of students, during their independent time, kept the telephone personnel busy answering questions. Groups, such as representatives from the community college and the Department of Labor and Industries can set up either in the main hall or in a conference room and have very busy days interviewing students who are interested and who wish to learn more about that specific activity. So many students responded when the Portland Community College people came that they called for additional personnel. We arranged individual conference space for each college person to have private interviews. Students came during their unscheduled time and kept the college people busy the entire day.

It is not unusual for the school to receive letters of appreciation from the invited groups after they have had a day of conferences at Marshall. They are impressed with the demeanor of the student body and the number of students who came for the interviews.

We are presently planning to provide still another link in our effort to help the child—that of having the counseling services available to the parents. In our community this can best be accomplished by evening conferences. We hope to have one evening when counselors and an administrator will be in their offices for conferences.

Since the inception of our new program, parent conferences have been requested much more frequently. Both the child and his parents profit from the opportunity of discussing the problems they are trying to resolve as a family. The counselor gains insight when he can observe the family as a unit.

It is evident that a Marshall counselor is a busy person, and will become even busier. We know that it is not realistic for him to expect to work individually with each counselee on a weekly schedule. We know that more must be done through student groups, with teachers, and with parents. Our counselors need more training if they are to be as successful with groups as they are with individuals.

For the emotionally disturbed child, more specialized services must be available. Marshall has a psychiatric social worker one day a week. He is invaluable, for he works with the counselors as well as with the counselees; but we need him on a full-time basis.

We also have a practicing psychologist one-half day a week. It is her responsibility to give projective tests and to confer with parent and child. Obviously a half day a week is not enough time for a student body of twenty-two hundred.

Our nurse is in the building only a half day a week. She is much in demand by students and by counselors who refer students to her.

In a system in which students have independent time, and thus more opportunity to communicate with others and to learn more about themselves, the counseling services should become the focal point for information and exploration in the search for self-evaluation.

THE ACTIVITY PROGRAM

It is in point, perhaps, to survey briefly the student activity program in those areas affected by the modular-flexible design. In September, 1963, when Marshall began the computerized modular-flexible program, almost the entire emphasis was placed on the development and refinement of the new instructional design. Teachers and administrators were deeply involved in the problems that had to be met with team teaching, large-group presentations, small-group techniques, and the use of independent-study time.

Students, however, became aware of the possibilities of an interesting "by-product" of the program. They soon discovered that many of their extracurricular small groups could meet during the day during their independent time. Thus class officers, executive cabinets, Girls' League representatives, honor society officers, and many others met during the school day to plan their activities. The honor society, for example, does all its planning, writing speeches, and practicing for the installation ceremonies during school time. Large projects like decorating for the Christmas formal, senior prom, and Rose Festival (a very important activity for the local citizenry) are also planned well ahead of deadlines. Students find that independent time gives them opportunities to serve in their activities during the school day without losing time from part-time jobs after school.

Students also were the first to challenge the "inflexibility" of the assembly schedule. From 1963 through the academic year 1965–1966, we scheduled the first hour on Fridays for extracurricular activities, particularly of an all-school nature. All class meetings, school elections, and the endless school forms that have to be filled out, as well as the regular school assembly program, had to be worked into that one period of three modules on Friday morning. After three years with a set time for assemblies and year-class meetings, we moved to a B schedule, with each module shortened by two minutes. The time thus saved provides for an assembly period. In this way we can have assemblies any day of the week, which gives the kind of flexibility deemed desirable for our assembly-type activities and still maintains the integrity of the instructional program. The second year in the new program we experimented with using the first module on Tuesday for carrying out the "business of running a large school." We discovered that by using the short registration (home room) period plus the one module, effective pep assemblies could be planned, class meetings could be held, and the usual forms could be filled out.

An encouraging development which would appear to be the result of growing student responsibility—a key objective of our program—has manifested itself in greater student involvement in the total school program. An example of this was a student-created student union board. This group met during independent time and after school hours to work on solving problems of student adjustment from a traditional to a modular schedule. Another group, called AIM (Association for the Improvement of Marshall), was formed to promote interest in class elections and general interest for school government.

We felt much progress was being made by students to assume their own leadership toward developing an awareness of their individual responsibility for solving school problems.

Since the fourth year in the new design, the senior class has served as hall monitors. Seniors carry identification cards, which give them the privilege of being in the halls at all times. They are expected, however, to keep the halls quiet and clear of all underclassmen except during the four-minute passing time between modules.

Other interesting and worthwhile projects, perhaps more of a curricular rather than extracurricular nature, include seniors who work in freshman classes as aides and a number of students who work with teachers in the primary grades of nearby schools.

In our flexible program, students can carry a full program and still find time during the school day to participate in programs of their own creation, thus becoming more adult citizens.

It is important to keep in mind that from an adult—even a teacher's—point of view, the effectiveness of the academic program may be the criteria for evaluating a school, especially one such as Marshall, where great emphasis is placed on innovations in the field of curriculum and instructional methodology. However, no system is exceptional unless the students themselves feel that they belong and that they have a vital part in not only the curriculum but in activities, too. They must be proud to be members of the student body.

School spirit often determines the success or failure of the curriculum, and never was it more true than at Marshall. Good student leadership, willingness on the part of the individual student to help implement the projects initiated by the leaders, and a sincere feeling that no problem is too large to be worked out when all are interested come only when the student honestly feels that it is his school.

Much of the success of the Marshall program can be attributed to the effective teamwork among students, faculty, parents, and administration. The carryover of student responsibility for himself and his learning to that of a genuine concern and responsibility for the total school program is slowly but surely manifesting itself at Marshall High School.

11

Validation of the New Design

Gaynor Petrequin

Computerized modular-flexible scheduling has allowed for reorganization within the school, reorganization that was virtually impossible with the traditional scheduling methods used. The preceding chapters have been an attempt to relate what has happened in a single secondary school as a result of modular-flexible scheduling.

The results to date make us feel quite optimistic that we are providing a much improved educational program for students than we were able to under the many restrictions of the former traditional schedule. To be able to provide positive statistical evidence substantiating our professional judgment to the satisfaction of all educators or laymen is another matter, however.

THE PROBLEM OF EVALUATION

Validation of any educational program must be in terms of the objectives of that program. Comparison of the results of one program against another, even if goals are quite similar, is exceedingly difficult if not impossible under the existing limitations of measuring instruments, considering the number of variables which affect the results.

As behavioral scientists and educators are well aware, an attempt to measure a variety of human behavioral manifestations with any degree of accuracy within the present sophistication of the science of measurement is a very precarious endeavor at best.

Each school district rightfully subscribes to its own unique set of goals. In most large districts, there is even flexibility for local school variations within the general goals of that district in order to meet the needs of its unique student body. Even if goals are found to be identical, the emphasis on specific goals or the importance ascribed to specific objectives will in all probability not be identical.

When the variables of school population and teacher variation are added, the likelihood that two separate schools can be compared as to the effectiveness of the same educational program is highly questionable. These facts, well known to educators, are not generally understood by school patrons. In some instances this lack of understanding has resulted in the effectiveness of one school system being compared with another, with the predetermined results "proved" by the group responsible for this kind of unscientific comparison.

Perhaps the greatest obstacle to the assessment of a modular program, with all its innovative components, as compared with the traditional program is that the former usually stresses behavioral goals, which cannot be measured validly by instruments designed primarily to measure knowledge or subject-matter goals.

The Marshall modular-flexible program has as its overall purpose the improvement of teaching and learning over that which we found possible in the lockstep format of a conventional program. The attainment of this general goal is accomplished by stressing the individual student—by individualizing teaching and learning as described in the preceding chapters.

Specifically some of our major objectives—in addition to the acquisition of factual knowledge needed to develop concepts and generalizations, and the development of communication and interpersonal skills needed for effective functioning in a world society—are the following:

1. To develop within each student the ability to accept responsibility for his own learning and, it is hoped, to develop responsible behavior and self-discipline in other areas of life
2. To develop within each student the ability to engage in honest and critical self-evaluation of his own capabilities, efforts, achievement, and goals
3. To develop within each student according to his ability intellectual inquiry, love of learning, creativity, divergent thinking and critical analysis, increased awareness of alternatives and the selection of appropriate ones, initiative and decision-making capabilities, problem-solving competencies, and respect for others and their opinions and feelings
4. To provide opportunity for each student to attain an excellence in his own way and in whatever area he wishes or is equipped to do so

Even if our graduates could be measured with some degree of accuracy, in terms of their attainment of the above objectives, we would still not be able to prove that they had more nearly attained these goals than they would have under a traditional school program.

Perhaps the most scientific method of determining the effectiveness of one educational program over another with identical goals would be to design a statistical comparative study with an adequate statistical sample of students from each program. Students in the two groups would have to be matched as to significant variable characteristics such that the two groups would be as similar as possible in all variables except for the variable tested (the educational program). However, to secure human beings nearly perfectly matched in background, ability, and present state of development, with similar out-of-school experiences, and to divide them in two groups—both with identical educational goals, mostly of a behavioral nature—and then to test for the attainment of these goals on validly and reliably designed objective-type instruments is a costly, laborious, and time-consuming endeavor in the field of psychological and educational research. In addition, the teacher variability between the two groups would somehow have to be reduced to a common denominator in order to make the study valid. Thus, at best, the feasibility of such a study to compare the effectiveness of a modular-flexible program with a traditional one is highly questionable.

The behavioral goals sought under the present Marshall modular program of course include cognitive goals which can be measured, at least in part, through the use of standardized achievement tests and by locally constructed teacher tests in the various curricular areas. Thus, an assessment of the new design in the dimension of subject-matter "achievement" is not only possible but relatively easy to do in contrast to measuring for other goals, particularly in the affective domain.

ACHIEVEMENT TEST EVIDENCE

Reports from our teachers comparing student achievement under the two different programs have varied. During the first year of the new design, some results were significantly better; others were not as good. It should be noted that during the first year, 1963–1964, a number of crucial problems existed both in the computer programming and in the implementation of the new concepts by the teaching staff, which adversely affected the school program. For the most part these early problems have been resolved. Generally, over the past four years teachers have become convinced that attainment of skills and general achievement is at least as high as previously, and probably higher. In a number of notable instances, teachers have reported significantly higher achievement in terms of subject-matter goals than under traditional programming; however, no claim is made here that these results are directly related to modular scheduling. They might very well be, but in some instances they may be affected by such variables as differences in classes or the general upgrading of the curricular and instructional programs.

Studies have been conducted to determine relative standings of Marshall students to those in the other eleven Portland schools on standardized city-wide achievement tests. Means were compared prior to the new design and, so far, for four years on the new program. The growth in achievement between the freshman and junior years, when the tests are administered, was also compared. Complications in assessment became evident as a change in the kinds of achievement tests administered occurred at the same time the new program was adopted. However, comparisons were made where possible relying on the professional judgment of the district's testing and research departments. In general, it can be safely said that as far as measurement through the use of standardized achievement tests is concerned, Marshall students are learning as much—and in one area, reading—significantly more than their counterparts did under the former traditional program.

At the present time, an extensive study is being conducted by the district's testing department with the collaboration of the School of Education at Stanford University. This study will evaluate the progress of individual students as compared with comparable students in other Portland high schools. This may prove to be a significant indication of the progress of Marshall students; but again it will measure only the traditional subject-matter-type objectives and will not reveal progress in the more elusive domains of behavior, which educators generally agree is the most important and the most difficult to assess.

LOCAL STUDIES AND INVESTIGATIONS

Throughout the past four years, many local studies were performed by school or district personnel. These included studies of grades, dropouts, student attitudes, teacher attitudes, student use of time, use of resources and instructional materials, follow-up of graduates, independent-study activities, small-group activities, and the like.

As was expected, grade and dropout studies have shown no significant differences over the traditional program. A depth statistical study of student attitudes regarding education, school, teachers, and aspects of modular programming has been conducted each year since 1963–1964. This has proved to be an interesting and informative project. Investigations and studies involving the new concepts such as independent study, small-group techniques, and teacher and student use of unstructured time have invariably revealed more favorable attitudes and commitment to learning and the modular program than even the teaching staff had expected.

Yearly follow-ups of our graduates indicate the large majority of those attending universities and other post-high-school training institutions believe that the modular program—with its emphasis on student responsibility, decision making, and the use of unstructured time—has given them better preparation for college than would otherwise be the case, as they compare their matriculation into college life with that of students from traditional high schools.

In short, of the many investigations including several sophisticated studies conducted by the Marshall or district staffs, all have revealed positive reaction to the new design and evidence indicating we are making the progress expected toward the realization of our goals.

STUDENT AND PARENT REACTION

During the 1963–1964 school year, two student surveys were conducted at different times by the executive cabinet of the student body to ascertain student reaction to the new program. Both surveys showed almost identical results. Approximately 89 percent of the students favored the new program over the old. This included freshmen—who had not experienced any other—and of course sophomores, juniors, and seniors—who had experienced one, two, and three years, respectively, of traditional structure.

During the year 1966–1967, a number of student committees visited traditional high schools in the Portland area for a full day to experience the traditional school program, with which they were not personally familiar. Each report was practically unanimous in praise of the Marshall program in contrast to the traditional. Many students who took part in these visitations expressed amazement at the many restrictions in learning opportunities and student decision making in the conventional programs.

Although our patrons have never been formally surveyed, their support of our endeavors has continually been felt by reactions of the Parent-Teachers Association, the Dads' Club, and many individual parents. This is not to say there are not parents who know "this program is not good for my child." At least 90 percent of this kind of comment are from parents whose youngsters have had problems in a traditional program or in elementary school and are having similar problems with us. Whereas formerly the teacher was frequently blamed as the source of the youngster's problem, now the new program has gained this distinction. At any rate, this is the initial reaction of many parents whose children have become involved in some type of school difficulty. Sometimes they are absolutely correct. If the student had been under the direct supervision of a teacher during the entire school day, he might not have become involved. As educators, however, we feel a good educational design for 90 percent of the students should not be sacrificed for the 10 percent or so who lack adequate self-discipline. Perhaps part of the educative process for the small minority ought to be in terms of learning responsible behavior by making choices and suffering the consequences of selecting inappropriate alternatives.

We do not wish to imply that we are ignoring those youngsters who cannot adjust to our (or probably any) school program. The services of the resource-center laboratory for assisting these students were discussed in the chapter on resource centers.

It is perhaps appropriate at this point to discuss briefly one of our more sophisticated studies, which is aimed directly at solving the problem of the student who is not making effective use of his unstructured time. This two-year project, funded by the Educational Grants Division of the Charles F. Kettering Foundation's Institute for Development of Educational Activities, is nearing completion at this time.

It is a two-phase project which endeavors to identify specific identification criteria for students who will in all probability not be able to use their independent-study time profitably when they enter a program similar to ours. The second phase will indicate a variety of field-tested treatments which can be utilized to change the student's behavioral patterns to that of responsible self-discipline, particularly as applies to use of his independent-study time.

The final report of this study is projected for release by the Institute for Development of Educational Activities in the fall of 1968. It is expected to be a notable contribution to schools moving into independent-study programs for all students.

Our present experimental training program to inculcate these desirable behaviors is a convincing argument when discussing the value of our program with parents who feel their youngsters need more supervision than they would normally receive in an independent-study situation.

Community reaction to modular scheduling can be ascertained somewhat by the very few parents in our district who request their youngsters be permitted to enter or to transfer to a conventional Portland high school. Also, there are those few families, that come to our attention, who move into the Marshall district specifically so their children can take advantage of our instructional system. It may be appropriate to describe an interesting, although unusual, case in this respect.

A knowledgeable parent living in a small town in southeastern Washington, influenced by the writings of J. Lloyd Trump and others, conducted a personal on-the-spot investigation of our program in the spring of 1964. The next September her two youngsters, a freshman boy and junior girl, registered at Marshall along with two of their friends from the same town. Although the family still maintained residence in Washington, where the father worked, they purchased a home in the Marshall district in which the mother and four youngsters lived during the week. Friday after school they drove home to father, about a five-hour automobile drive one way, and returned to Portland Sunday evening. They remained in town only if the youngsters took part in Friday evening school activities or if the weather was too severe. The following year the second family moved to a rural area near Portland. These two youngsters now lived at home, but continued to attend Marshall, which cost the family over $1,100 per year tuition for the privilege. The first family maintained the commuting arrangement for three years. The sacrifices involved are obviously great. It does indicate the extent of commitment of two families to modular-flexible programming.

ASSESSING PROCESSES

An effective method of assessing a total innovative instructional program is to examine the components of that program or the processes utilized in the teaching and learning acts. These processes when evaluated in terms of the psychology of learning should be a meaningful indication of effectiveness. Thus, a brief review of the four teaching-learning modes which characterize the Marshall program, and most modular programs, in terms of good learning theory would be appropriate.

Chapter 2 points out the place of the large-group presentation as a teaching mode. There are times when the teacher "presents" or talks to students in any teaching situation. A number of studies have shown that the average teacher talks well over 50 percent of the time in a traditional classroom. Would it not be more efficient and effective to prepare a good presentation to be given at one time to 150 students rather than five times a day to 30 students each time, as is done in the traditional school? The same may be asked about showing a film or utilizing an outside resource speaker. The time saved by the teacher in making the one presentation rather than five would be utilized in preparing a first-rate presentation and in working with students in other learning activities which are costly in time but effective in learning.

The point was well made by a chemistry teacher in a traditional Portland high school who expressed frustration under the lockstep by having to "pre-lab an experiment five times on Monday, rushing the students to perform the experiment in too little time on Tuesday, and then post-labing it five times on Wednesday."

A similar examination of the small-group learning mode points up the advantage of this phase of learning over that of the traditional classroom. It is well known that learning occurs best when the learner becomes personally involved. The primary purpose of the small group is discussion and interaction. In a conventional class of thirty students, the skillful teacher may engage a third of the students in discussion. In a small group of six to fifteen students, the nonparticipant is conspicuous. Involvement then in the typical small group is much greater than in the traditional classroom.

The laboratory phase—learning by doing—occurs in both traditional and modular programs. The student in the modular program has the advantage, however, since his laboratory period is structured in length to the unique requirements of the course, and in addition, he has access to the laboratory during most of his unstructured time to work at his own pace.

Undoubtedly, the greatest advantage to the learner in a modular-flexible design is his independent-study time, in which he determines his activities according to his unique requirements. The many productive activities possible during independent time, as discussed in Chapters 4 and 5, are without doubt far greater than available in the traditional "study hall."

The learner's superior posture in a modular-flexible program has been similarly determined by the secondary education department in Stanford University's School of Education. The Stanford evaluation study was predominantly one of investigating the processes of teaching and learning under both traditional and modular programs.

For example, it was determined reliably that the Marshall staff of ninety-two teachers, exclusive of counselors and administrators, conduct approximately 1,083 individual-student conferences in a typical week, or 15 per teacher per week. In contrast, schools not yet on modular scheduling have indicated a much smaller number. Figure 11-1 is an analysis of teacher-student conferencing at Marshall.

In short, the Stanford study indicates a much more effective use of teacher and student time under modular programming in terms of accepted laws of learning.

PROFESSIONAL ASSESSMENT

Validation of our innovative educational program and of modular programming specifically can probably best be done by the professional judgment of the educational community. What do the educators working in the program day after day think of it as

Following are the results of the data collected from teachers, excluding counselors, administrators and librarians, over a five month period of time. Each teacher reported on a different day of the week, once a month over a five month period.

	November	December*	January	February	March*
Type of conference:					
Total individual	295	165	241	197	179
Total small groups (2-5)	42	31	39	40	34
Total small groups (6-15)	2	1	2	9	3
Total larger than 15	1	1	1	1	2
Conferences requested by:					
Teacher	135	74	101	87	85
Student	205	124	182	151	131
Administrator/counselor	–	–	–	7	2
Parent	–	–	–	2	–
Time of conference:					
Before school	19	11	10	11	13
During school	299	179	254	221	196
After school	22	8	19	15	9
Reason for conference:					
Academic work	219	129	178	125	141
Attendance	29	14	23	32	15
College planning	5	2	5	5	1
Discipline	23	7	15	10	19
Extra or co-curr. act.	34	39	29	49	26
Personal	29	15	30	21	13
Program change/planning	9	5	3	4	8
Student part. in school gov.	3	6	6	–	–
Vocational planning	5	3	6	5	2
Work experience	6	4	6	6	3
Other (misc.)	12	6	10	9	4

(Occasionally more than one reason was given for a single conference.)

	November	December*	January	February	March*
Total time per day for all teachers spent in conferencing	62 hrs. 5 min.	35 hrs. 11 min.	58 hrs. 52 min.	53 hrs. 38 min.	47 hrs. 44 min.
Average time per teacher per day spent in conferencing	40 min.	39 min.	38 min.	35 min.	39 min.
Average number of conferences per day per teacher	3.5	3.8	3.04	2.68	3

*According to the statistical design only 54 teachers reported in December and 73 in March because of holidays. In all other months, the total number of teachers included in the reporting was 92.

FIGURE 11-1. Teacher-student conference analysis, 1966-1967

compared with their former traditional experiences? What do the educators who have seen the program in action and have studied it in depth think of it? What do the eminent educational theorists in the leading schools of education believe?

Surveys were, of course, conducted and statements were collected from the Marshall faculty from time to time to elicit their professional assessment. Results were always strongly in favor of the new design. Through the end of the fourth year, eight teachers had asked for and secured transfers to conventional high schools within the district because of their lack of complete acceptance of the philosophy on which it is based.

A significant statement was submitted on October 1, 1963, a month into the program, by an art instructor, a recognized master teacher with several decades of successful teaching and the oldest teacher on the staff. Her complete statement is reproduced exactly as she submitted it.

> My program and class load is as near ideal as possible. I have always thought students and teachers needed a "coffee break"—not, however, such long unsupervised "breaks" as freshmen and sophomores are taking.
>
> I have 6 classes this year and feel none of the pressure I have felt in previous years with 5 classes. Meeting fewer people in longer sessions seems to eliminate the "rat race" feeling. Students are doing as well and as much work in the two long sessions as they did in the 5 short sessions. In general, students seem more enthusiastic about art classes—they seem anxious to work.

Thousands of educators have visited the school in the past five years. Their unsolicited evaluations are certainly an indication of the education profession's opinion. These have been overwhelmingly favorable to the theory and practice of our new instructional system. There are numerous documented instances of schools adapting their own unique form of modular programming as the result of their study of the Marshall program.

To allude to any of the recognized authorities in secondary education, particularly in the fields of curriculum and instruction, would be redundant. Their presentations to professional groups and their writings are well known. They abound with the urging for responsible change and a discarding of the lockstep appropriate to the "horse and buggy age."

It is sometimes irksome, however, to be challenged by one's conservative colleagues to "prove" that "your system is better than mine." The burden of proof always falls on the innovator, and perhaps this is as it should be. These conservative critics will not accept the professional judgment of the field practitioners as validation of innovative practices, although the only way they assess their schools is by their own professional judgment. They insist on statistical studies or other "objective" data which they cannot provide even to support their own practices. Certainly, many practices found in traditional programs cannot be supported by research; in fact, many of them are contrary to research findings.

The feeling of the Marshall staff is probably best reflected in a statement from our science department. The statement summarizes the primary message of this chapter as well:

> From the teacher point of view, those of us in the science department are generally very happy with many of the aspects of the new program. We would not like to go back to the traditional fifty-five minute period, five days a week type of program. The longer laboratory periods are very valuable. The freedom that students have to come in and make up work, go over work again, add to their work and initiate new ideas is very valuable. The opportunity to have teacher-student conference time within the school day is helpful. The freedom and relaxation of the new program is valuable to us, and the teacher-to-teacher contact including the day-to-day critiques, either vocal or observed, of each others' work has helped us all to grow. Planning with each other, we have the combined strengths of at least two people's ideas whereas we used to have little more than our own ideas to call upon. The variety of the program from day to day is stimulating in itself. Problems have not disappeared, but we now have some new and better ways to attack them.

DIRECTIONS FOR THE FUTURE

It is important to note that the modular-flexible program at Marshall, with its many innovations in curriculum and instructional methodology, is not a static program. Each year the members of the instructional staff restructure their courses in light of their past experience in order to continually improve the teaching-learning experiences. In addition, curricular offerings are continually examined in order to provide as meaningful and functional curricula as possible to meet the needs and interests of the wide range of our student population.

The preceding chapters have pointed out trends which have developed through several years, particularly in teaching and learning strategies. Most important in this respect has been the trend toward less formal structure in the program of the average and above-average student, and similarly there is diminishing structure from the freshman to the senior levels. Of at least equal importance is the growing significance of the independent-study activities. More and more emphasis is being given to this key concept of the program both by faculty and students.

A significant curricular development has been the initiation and growth of interdisciplinary offerings. Two outstanding examples are the humanities course for seniors and the power mechanics offering including science, language arts, and math, for non-college-bound students. The trend to break down the strict divisions between disciplines is quite apparent as teachers develop greater concern about the total effect of the high school curriculum on students.

Perhaps the most exciting development in both methodology and curriculum is the definite trend to "performance curriculum," often referred to as "continuous progress" or "non-gradeness." In the fourth year of the program, two electronics courses were taught completely as performance curriculum, in which each student progressed at his own rate working predominantly with "learning packages," or "unipaks." During the fifth year, the first-year algebra course was similarly offered. Developments along these lines are also apparent in English and social studies.

Undoubtedly a look into the future at Marshall High School would indicate an integration of the disciplines, centered for the most part on conceptual learning and the replacement of the criterion of *time* for the granting of credit to the criterion of *performance*.

One thing is certain, however, and that is change will continue—change directed to the goal of *individualization* of teaching and learning, so that the unique potential of each student will be developed just as far as possible within the parameters of human and material resources within which we are compelled to operate.